COMPLETE HISTORY OF THE
ROSICRUCIAN ORDER

By
H. SPENCER LEWIS, PH. D., F. R. C.
First Imperator of the Rosicrucian Order
for North and South America

THE BOOK TREE
San Diego, California

First published
1929
by The Rosicrucian Press, Ltd.
San Jose, California

ISBN 978-1-58509-201-7

Cover layout and design
by Toni Villalas

Published by
The Book Tree
P.O. Box 16476
San Diego, CA 92176
www.thebooktree.com

We provide fascinating and educational products to help awaken the public to new ideas and
information that would not be available otherwise.
Call 1 (800) 700-8733 for our *FREE BOOK TREE CATALOG*.

DEDICATION

▽

To the Memory of

BROTHER JULIUS SACHSE, F. R. C.
Historian,

*last descendant of the First American
Rosicrucian Colony, whose History of
their achievements will remain as a
monument to the Faith and Love of their
great leader, Magister Kelpius,*

THIS BOOK IS DEDICATED

*that I may place a flower among
the many at the side of
his grave.*

▽

FOREWORD

The author, a former high ranking Rosicrucian and prolific author on the subject for many years, reveals the true history of the Rosicrucian order. Many popular accounts put forth the idea that it was started in Germany in the seventeenth century by Christian Rosenkreuz, but Lewis shows how and why the order and its origins goes much further back into the past than this story relates. According to the author, there was simply a revival taking place in the seventeenth century that has continued on until today. Explore some of the world's most ancient mystical secrets, what they really mean, and why they were preserved for centuries by the Rosicrucians.

Paul Tice

CONTENTS

▽

PART ONE

COMPLETE AUTHENTIC HISTORY OF THE ROSICRUCIAN ORDER

CHAPTER   PAGE

Preface   17
Introduction   23
    I The Traditional History of the Order . .   33
   II The Growth of the Order in the Orient . .   61
  III The Work of the Disciples   75
   IV The 108-Year Cycle and "C. R-C." . . . 103
    V The Popular Revival in Germany 111
   VI The Birth of Semi-Rosicrucian Organizations 127
  VII The First Rosicrucians in America . . . 163
 VIII The Present Rosicrucian Order in America . 169
   IX International Jurisdiction of the Order . . 191
    X Development and Expansion in France . . 209
   XI Other World-Wide Rosicrucian Activities . 216
  XII Program of Decentralization 223

The True Name and Emblems of the
International Rosicrucian Order

Registered in the U. S. Patent Office
exclusively in the name of AMORC

MODERN SPHINX PRESERVES AGE-OLD PRINCIPLES

The former Imperator of the Rosicrucian Order, Dr. H. Spencer Lewis, in full ritualistic regalia, upon the occasion of the dedication of the Rose-Croix Science Building in A.D. 1934, is seen here depositing for posterity a scroll which contains fifteen of the Order's most important philosophic principles. On his left are Dr. Clement Le Brun, Past Grand Master of AMORC, and an assistant.

EXTENSION OF JURISDICTION

A decree by the F.U.D.O.S.I. and International Council of the Rose-Croix of the world, issued August 13, 1934, at Brussels, Belgium, empowering the A.M.O.R.C., as the authoritative Rosicrucian Order of the Western world, to extend its jurisdiction to include the countries and territories of South America.

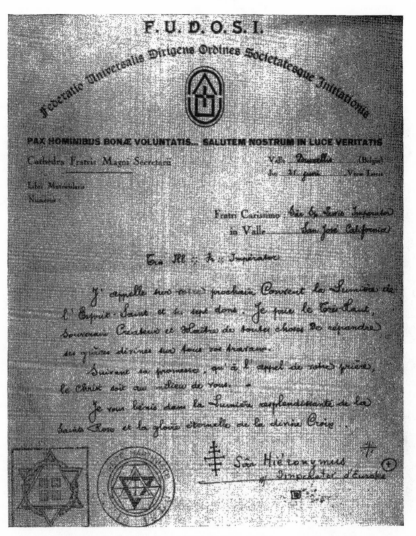

SALUTATIONS FROM THE IMPERATOR OF EUROPE

A communication from Sar Hieronymus, Imperator of the Rose-Croix of Europe to the first Imperator of AMORC of North and South America, Dr. H. Spencer Lewis, extending greetings. The felicitations were written on the official stationery of the F.U.D.O.S.I., a federation of the authoritative, initiatory and mystical Orders of the world, AMORC being the only Rosicrucian movement of the Western world affiliated with it at that time.

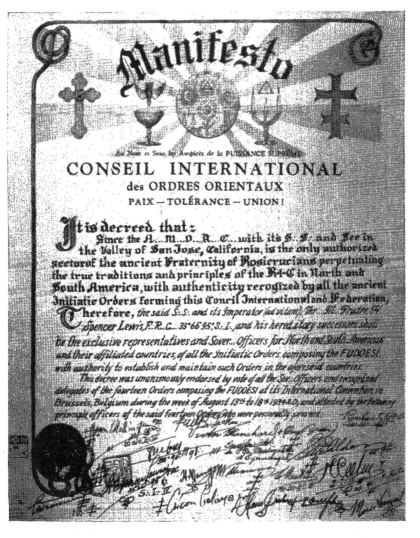

AUTHORITATIVE RECOGNITION

Manifesto issued and signed by the highest dignitaries of the International Council of the Rosicrucian Order for the world, at a conclave of the F.U.D.O.S.I. held in Brussels, Belgium, during the week of August 13 to 18, 1934 A.D. The Manifesto decrees that the AMORC, with See in San Jose, California, is the authorized sector of the ancient Rosicrucian fraternity in North and South America.

MEDITATION CAVE

Fleeing religious intolerance in Europe and looking toward America as a land of freedom of conscience, a group of Rosicrucians under the leadership of Master Johannes Kelpius settled on the banks of Wissahickon Creek in Pennsylvania in the year 1694. This was the beginning of the first cycle of the Rosicrucian Order in the New World. Johannes Kelpius, leading a life of celibacy, frequently lived as an ascetic for months at a time in the above cave. The cave is now part of the celebrated Fairmount Park in Philadelphia.

(Photo by AMORC)

EARLY ROSICRUCIAN SETTLEMENT

In Ephrata, Pennsylvania, in the early eighteenth century, this settlement of Rosicrucians and mystics was established by Johann Conrad Beissel. The edifice to the left above is the *Saron,* or Sisters' House. Adjoining it is the *Saal,* or Temple. There are other edifices not shown, and there were others that have since passed with time. Many of the settlers were descendants of the earlier Rosicrucian colony established in Philadelphia in 1694 by Johannes Kelpius.

ANCIENT RITUALISTIC POSTURE

This ancient figure of a prince, possibly the son of King Mena of the first dynasty (3400 B.C.), assumes a ritualistic posture familiar to all Rosicrucian lodge and chapter members. The position of the hands and the wearing of the apron reveal the early origin of the symbolic gesture. The prince was undoubtedly attached to one of the mystery schools of the period. This rare figure, found in a tomb at Abydos, is one of several thousand authentic objects on display in the Rosicrucian Egyptian, Oriental Museum.

PREFACE

The mystery which has always surrounded the origin and history of the Great White Brotherhood has probably been one of its fascinating attractions, even with those who had no interest in its teachings or activities. The mystery is not eliminated by a revelation of the *real* as well as the *traditional* facts associated with its origin; and in its history one will find romance, intrigue, astounding achievements, fascinating exploits, and alluring inducements.

The history of the Brotherhood must be divided into two general classifications. First, that which is traditional, and which has come down to the present time by word of mouth, supported by more or less definite references in ancient writings or symbolical passages in the rituals or teachings; and second, that which is truly historical and supported by the records found in the various branches of the organization throughout the world.

It is realized that the traditional history of the organization is very often cast aside, or accepted with considerable doubt by those who hesitate to believe in the antiquity of the organization. Persons of this type prefer to have the history of the organization begin with its first definite, printed records. They forget that everything of human construction had a beginning, and that there must have been an origin and beginning of the Order which antedates the first definite, printed or written records.

It was generally believed, several hundred years ago, that the *historical birth* of the Rosicrucians did not antedate the seventeenth century. It was likewise believed that the *traditional birth* of the Order began some time in the Christian Era, and ended at the time of the historical birth. In other words, the attitude was taken that all the stories, reports, and references to the Rosicrucians as existing prior to the seventeenth century belonged to the *traditional history* of the Order. But, the many discoveries of documents, books, manuscripts, and references of an authentic nature in the past century have taken the actual origin and existence of the Order backward step by step, year by year, into the very heart of the so-called traditional period.

The demand on the part of Rosicrucian students throughout the world, and the search on the part of thousands of others, for more facts regarding both the traditional and actual periods of the Order's existence, have warranted this history.

Parts of this history appeared for the first time in the official Rosicrucian magazine called the *American Rosae Crucis,* beginning with the January, 1916, issue. That history was, at that time, considered the most complete outline of the traditional part of the Order's existence ever presented, and has been widely utilized by other writers who found therein the clues which enabled them to verify many of the statements made. Since 1916 a number of other histories have appeared in the French, Dutch, German, and English languages by eminent officers of the organization. In most of these, the facts presented in the articles which appeared in the *American Rosae Crucis* have been utilized and appreciation expressed for the publication of hitherto concealed records.

The present history is an extension of the one published in the magazine, and is considerably augmented by documents, books, and papers sent to the author by other historians or members of foreign branches of the Order, who were able to find further details because of the clues given in the original articles. Credit must also be given to the researches made by the official historian of the Order in America, *Fra Fidelis,* who, through his editorial association with one of the largest newspapers in North America, and his connections with the Order and with foreign libraries and records in many languages, has been able to make extensive researches covering a number of years, thereby bringing to light many important and intensely interesting facts.

Whether one accepts all of the points of the traditional history or not, one is certain to feel that the origin of what is now the Rosicrucian Order is found in the early mystery schools of the Great White Brotherhood. A study of the schools of philosophy and arcane wisdom in the Oriental lands preceding the Christian Era reveals that there is but one land in which the Rosicrucian organization could have had its birth. That land is Egypt; and even the casual student of Egyptian history is impressed with the probability of the birth of the organization in that land.

If one sets aside the traditional history entirely, and accepts only that which is based upon very definite records in printed or official manuscript form, one must reject the popular and entirely fictitious claim that the Rosicrucian Order had its origin in the seventeenth century in Germany. The very positive references to the Order in printed books dated centuries earlier in other lands prove conclusively that the Order was very old and very well established when it had a form of revival in Germany in the seventeenth century. Likewise, one discovers at once that the romantic or symbolic story regarding *Christian Rosenkreuz* and *his* foundation of the first Rosicrucian body must be rejected, unless one associates that story with similar stories found in many earlier records.

The author, therefore, presents the following history as the most modern version, and perhaps the most complete outline of the history of the Rosicrucian Order, with the hope that the members of the Order will find between the lines the facts which are carefully concealed; and the inquiring mind, seeking for a mystery story and nothing more, will also find in the printed words a mystical romance prepared to his liking.

INTRODUCTION

It is no violation of secrecy to give the outer, objective details of the various activities of the Great White Brotherhood, but the genuine conservatism of the Eastern Councils until recent years has acted as a barrier against such publicity as we in America and the West generally believe necessary for the growth of any public or semipublic institution.

After twenty years' study of the doctrines and principles and a very careful examination of all matters pertaining to the history of the Order, one does not find a single prohibition against the general publication of the history except in such minor details as are closely associated with the working or manifestation of some of the R. C. doctrines. While these exceptions are few, although of vast importance to the higher students, they have undoubtedly caused the subconscious attitude on the part of all R. C. Fratres and Sorores that it is safer, in the face of their individual sacred oaths, to refrain from all mention of either the antiquity or progression of the Order.

There is also the element of mysticism which explains the attitude of even the most advanced Fratres and Sorores. Realizing, as most of them do, that the complete history of the Brotherhood has never been given to the public and has for centuries defied the casual researches of scientists, historians and archivists alike, they feel a certain pride in having been able to mystify the profoundly inquisitive minds. Even the grossly erroneous and biased *resumé* of the history of the Brotherhood given in various encyclopedias, reference books, and histories only adds to this feeling of pride and victory.

Such secrecy is not only uncalled for but is positively detrimental to the Order. We have a natural antipathy toward that which may be characterized as "mystically mythical"; and precisely such is the general impression of the origin and existence of the R. C. Order in the minds of many thousands today.

Nor is it necessary to enshroud the history of the Order with a cloak of blackest mystery to make the Order itself appeal to the thinking mind. One will find that the true history of the Order arouses, even commands, such deep respect for its noble birth, grand growth, and wonderful increase of power, that this is a greater attraction to the thinking mind than the element of mystery.

Inexactness and indefiniteness are the principal faults to be found with most all the published accounts of the original and present status of the Order. The few instances of wilful and inconsistent deception shown by some writers on the subject may be ignored in any consideration of the matter, for no mind can explain these things nor account for them, aside from the writer's own personal bias which we are always led to believe has had no influence upon the honesty of the work.

Still, there are many very definite and exact facts easily within the reach of an analytical mind bent upon historical research, even when that mind is uninitiated into the secrets of the Order.

The claim has been made that the AMORC is the oldest fraternal or secret order known to man. This claim makes the Order antedate Freemasonry and the latter has always claimed great antiquity. Here again the investigator is confronted with a mass of details purporting to be the history of Freemasonry, but gradually classifying itself into two groups which one may label "facts" and "traditions."

On the point of its connection with the Rosicrucians, Freemasonry is more or less silent. It traces its antiquity to Solomon's Temple, and refers to characters whose history, if not actual existence, is

cloaked with mystery. Its published history is very esoteric and mystical, although its actual history, as known to all advanced Rosicrucians, is a living testi-
' monial to the truth of the notable principles of Brotherhood which actuate Freemasonry.

So closely are the two Orders allied in some lands that many of the great exponents of the one are active workers in the other. Freemasonry has acknowledged its debt to the ancient White Brotherhood by adding a Rosicrucian Degree to the Ancient and Accepted Scottish Rite.

H. SPENCER LEWIS, F. R. C.

ADDENDUM

The author of this work passed through transition (the Rosicrucian term for that change from mortal to immortal existence commonly referred to as death) on Wednesday, August 2, 1939, in San Jose, California, the See of the Rosicrucian Order. For a quarter of a century he devoted his time and genius exclusively to the furtherance of Rosicrucian doctrine in the Americas. He was unstinting in the sacrifices he made (as had been the venerable masters before him) that Rosicrucian idealism might survive and its heritage of wisdom be transmitted to the searching and inquiring minds of men and women, so that their lives might accordingly be bettered. Also, like the leaders of the Rosicrucian Order in past centuries, he was Cosmically prepared, if not ordained for his tremendous task, with a versatility of talents amounting to genius, and an abundance of dynamic energy.

There is no greater testimony of his abilities and powers of accomplishment, than that in so few years he should make an organization, the name and repute of which had been commonly confined to dusty tomes and the records of secret archives, come to command the attention and respect of thousands of persons in every walk of life, and in every section of North and South America. There was hardly any realm of creative enterprise which his mind and personality did not touch. The technical diagrams used to illustrate the precepts of the Rosicrucian teachings, as well as the elaborate symbolical paintings which ornamented the periodicals of the Order, issued for membership and for public consumption alike, were the products of his artistic ability. Many of the Temples of the Rosicrucian Lodges throughout this jurisdiction of the Order are examples of his skill of design and mastery of color harmony in ornamentation. In the Sanctums and homes of members, and in some of the edifices of the See of the Order are large oil paintings executed by him. Likewise, the very architecture and structural design of these buildings are the results of his creative efforts.

Scientifically accurate, insofar as their technical employment of physical laws is concerned, are the instruments and devices he invented and constructed to demonstrate nature's phenomena, that men might physically perceive and come to comprehend the majesty of the Cosmic laws he so loved. Such instruments included the Luxatone, a color organ, which demonstrated the relationship of sound and color years before such present instruments were constructed. The Planetarium projector, which he designed and erected for astronomical display and instruction, was the first instrument of its kind made entirely in America.

His knowledge of human nature, traits of character, and their relation to the everyday problems which beset people, made him much in demand as a *human engineer,* and a consultant upon personal welfare matters by societies and individuals. His executive ability and organizing genius made him, early in life, a success in the advertising and business worlds, a career which he forfeited for his higher obligation as Imperator of the Rosicrucian Order. He was much sought after by service clubs and business executives, as a counsellor in their respective fields. His literary talent is attested to in his numerous books on a variety of topics and his innumerable articles appearing in Rosicrucian periodicals throughout the world, and in technical and popular journals.

His self-sacrifices made him indifferent to wealth. His personal fortune and large sums of money which he came to command were devoted to furthering the Rosicrucian Order's expansion. Upon his transition, his personal estate was extremely modest in assets of any tangible nature. His sacrifices were not all material. The greatest he had to make at times was his peace of mind. He was, with the rise of Rosicrucian doctrine to prominence in the Western world, the personal target of every individual, society, or group which was envious of the Order or sought to suppress the knowledge it preserved. Their machinations were centered upon him, for with the cessation of his activities, they conceived the abolition of Rosicrucian philosophy. These forces which conspired against the Rosicrucian Order of the Twentieth Century were parallels of the same interests that sought to extirpate knowledge in the Middle Ages, and, in fact, in every era of civilization. Their reasons for seeking to do so were in some instances superstitious fear, in others misguided religious zeal, and more frequently the desire for power. His ordeal was one of vilification of character, calumny, and malicious persecution and harassment.

These torments, however, became a crucible out of which came forth a strong, resolute character. He lived to be recognized throughout the world, by the preceptors of the Rosicrucian Order and profane historians alike, as the greatest authority upon and master of the Rosicrucian teachings in modern times.

In accordance with his wish, the traditions of the Rosicrucian Order, its Constitution, and the vote of the Board of Directors of the Supreme Grand Lodge of AMORC, on August 12, 1939, authority was transmitted to his son, Ralph M. Lewis, to succeed him as Imperator.

All data and events chronicled in this work, subsequent to August 12, 1939, are by the incumbent Imperator of the AMORC for North and South America.

R. M. L.
February 10, 1941.

CHAPTER I

THE TRADITIONAL HISTORY OF
THE ORDER

HE Rosicrucian Order had its traditional conception and birth in Egypt in the activities of the Great White Lodge. In giving the story of the origin, the writer realizes that to an exceptional degree exactness will be demanded by the reader, and in return pardon must be granted for reiteration.

Space will not be used in describing conditions in Egypt as they existed at the time of the conception of so wonderful an organization as this. The reader is requested to read either a brief or extended history of Egypt, which will prove highly illuminating upon this subject.

One will find, however, that the Egyptians had reached a high state of civilization and advanced learning at the beginning of the XVIII dynasty, comparable only with the European Renaissance. Many were the means adopted to preserve the knowledge attained that it might be correctly given to future generations. The hieroglyphic markings on the pyramids, obelisks, and temple walls give us evidence of the first desires to make permanent the knowledge and learning of the Egyptians.

The more profound secrets of nature, science, and art were not to be entrusted to the masses, however, nor were they susceptible to preservation through writing upon papyri. For this reason classes were formed by the most learned, attended by the select minds, and there the doctrines and principles of science were taught.

These classes or *schools,* as history refers to them, were held in the most isolated grottos at times, and again in the quiet of some of the temples erected to the many Egyptian gods.

Actually, it is extremely difficult to determine when these schools began. The search for knowledge among the ancient Egyptians was undoubtedly coeval with their conscious observation and analysis of the current happenings of their lives and times. The cyclical repetitions of certain phenomena in nature and in their own beings were the first *mysteries* of early man. In fact, these things, to a great extent, still remain mysteries today. The personal mysteries—or rather the intimate ones—were those of birth and death, and that strange resurrection that occurred periodically in nature, as a rejuvenation of plant life in the spring.

At first, the term *mysteries* must have been synonymous with the unknown. Later it came to represent, to the Egyptian neophyte and priest alike, an uncommon or esoteric knowledge of the laws and purposes of life and being. Thus the appellation, *mystery school,* or place of imparting knowledge of the mysteries. Such first mysteries consisted of a matrix of mythology, founded on facts of observation and figments of imagination. From them evolved the indisputable truths of the inner comprehension of Cosmic law, just as there emerges from modern theories and hypotheses the eventual light of truth.

The first mystery schools were devoted principally to agrarian rites, such as the paying of homage to the fertility of the land, and the fecundity of domestic animals, and the offering of libations to the gods of the seasons. We might say that religion and learning formed the basic pattern of the instruction of the early mystery schools. The Osirian mysteries, deriving their name from the god, Osiris, of ancient Egypt, are credited with being one of the most popular expounded by the mystery schools. However, within its general ceremonies and rituals was the nebulous formation of *a vast philosophy of immor-*

tality, for it sought to embrace the welfare and future of the dead.

Osiris was the god of earth, the first substance from whence things sprang. He was likewise the symbol of *good* and was in constant conflict with the powers and forces of evil. The legends and myths declared that he was murdered by his brother Seth. He was later brought to life by the goddess Isis, and her son Horus, the latter symbolized by the bird, the hawk. Horus later, in turn, avenged Osiris by killing Seth. Crude as all of this may seem, in its telling, it had a far more important and mystical meaning. As Plutarch says: ". . . so the legend before us is a kind of reflection of a history reflecting the true meaning of other things; as is shown further by the sacrifices containing a representation of mourning and sadness; as also by the ground plan of the temples, in some parts spreading out into colonnades and courts open to the sky, and lightsome, in others having underground, hidden and dark galleries (like those at Thebes) and halls as well; . . ." In other words, the architecture of the temples of Egypt, the openness, the spaciousness, the lighted courtyards, on the one hand, and the underground passages, on the other, and certain dark and dreary places, represented the life and glory of Osiris, his death, his temporary stay in the nether world, then his glorious resurrection again.

Since Osiris was the judge in the after-world of the conduct of the dead who came before him, the plays of the mystery schools (for their truths were revealed as mystical dramas) attempted as well to define that moral conduct which is essential for the greater life after death. The priests and preceptors sought to teach lessons in each act of the mystery dramas. At the ancient temple of Dendera, the ritual was performed with puppets, perhaps the earliest record of the use of puppets. Each had its part to enact; even a miniature bier was constructed, upon which the effigy of Osiris was placed. This temple was first erected by Khufu, in 2900 B. C. In other temples, some of the ceremonies were enacted by persons who were carefully chosen for the roles, and intensively trained. Those who were to be initiated, or inducted into these mysteries—in other words, those who were the tyros, or candidates—were brought to the temple to witness the plays, after assuming certain very strict obligations. Frequently the rites were performed on a great, highly ornamented barge on the sacred lake, usually in moonlight. Herodotus tells us: "On this lake it is that the Egyptians represent by night his sufferings, whose name I refrain from mentioning (Osiris), and this representation they call their mysteries. I know well the whole course of the proceedings in these ceremonies, but they shall not pass my lips."*

Astronomical observations, or the mysteries of the heavens, found their place in the legends of Osiris as well. The days numbering the phases of the moon were related to the purported age of Osiris. It is not that the Egyptians actually believed that Osiris was a deified individual, or that he actually lived on earth a certain number of years, but to round out the legend he was given an age, and the age was related to observable phenomena, revealing further the fact that Osiris was an allegorical character representing truths or *mysteries*. Plutarch states: "The number of years that some say Osiris lived, others that he reigned, was eight and twenty; for just so many are the lights of the moon, and for so many days doth she revolve about the circle."**

The mystery schools of the old and middle kingdoms gradually experienced a transition from symbolical rites and dramatic rituals, to what we may term a philosophical analysis of the "physics"

---

*Herodotus, from *The Euterpé*.
**Plutarch—*Isis and Osiris*.

of the earth and of man's material nature, as well as such considerations as life after death. In other words, physical philosophy, or what rightly may be termed *scientific conjecture* began to hold forth with religion and mysticism. For example, the sistrum is an ancient device consisting of an oval, or round frame, in which are inserted little movable beads or rods, and to which a straight handle is affixed at one end. When it is shaken, these beads and rods vibrate, and it serves as a rattle. In the earliest periods of Egypt's history, and later during its decadence when the custom revived, this device was shaken so that the noise it emitted would frighten off evil spirits. However, at the height of the greatest culture and *secret learning* of the mystery schools, it became a symbol of universal or *Cosmic motion.* It was conceived that all things that are must be *shaken,* must be kept in *motion* by nature, if they are to generate themselves. If their motion ceases, so then shall they. We see here, then, that a thousand years before the earliest Greek atomic theories were advanced, a doctrine of *motion,* as the generation or cause of all matter, was expounded.

That portion of this vast knowledge which has been transmitted to us as inscriptions in stone, or on parchment, is a negligible part of the whole.

There was a wealth of knowledge, an accumulation of perhaps centuries, the result of numerous investigations, tedious and heart-rending probing into nature's secrets, the significance of which the Kheri Heb (the High Priest or temple master) alone knew. The fear to entrust this knowledge to any kind of tangible form that could be abased by wrongdoers, into whose possession it might fall, is one motive, and a most logical one, for imparting it only by *word of mouth*—to those worthy. Those who doubt that such a knowlege ever existed—and was transmitted by mouth to ear—because there is no original manuscript, papyrus, or stele to substantiate it, are themselves ignorant of the mundane, historic evidence which gives weight to this belief. No less an authority than Egyptologist Sir E. A. Wallis Budge states: "It is impossible to doubt that these were 'mysteries' in the Egyptian religion, and this being so, it is impossible to think that the highest order of the priests did not possess esoteric knowledge which they guarded with the greatest care. Each priesthood, if I read the evidence correctly, possessed a 'Gnosis', a 'superiority of knowledge', which they never did put into writing, and so were enabled to enlarge or diminish its scope as circumstances made necessary. It is therefore absurd to expect to find in Egyptian papyri descriptions of the secrets which formed the esoteric knowledge of the priests. Among the 'secret wisdom' of the priests must be included the knowledge of which day was the shortest of the year, i. e., the day when OSIRIS died and the new sun began his course, and the day when SIRIUS would rise heliacally, and the true age of the moon, and the days when the great festivals of the year were to be celebrated."*

If the *secret wisdom* was imparted in any tangible form, it is to be found to exist in the symbolism of the Egyptians, namely, in such devices as were not an integral part of their language or common writing. In this manner, a symbol would exoterically depict to one mind one meaning, and to another a far different significance. This is not merely a supposition, but a fact borne out by such a vast number of circumstances and indications, as to remove them from the realm of coincidence. It will suffice to mention but one such example. The Egyptian ground plans of a temple were almost always oblong in shape. Likewise this sign ☐ was a symbol in Egypt of the letter "M," or "Ma," implying the earth or

*Sir E. A. Wallis Budge, former keeper of the Department of Egyptian Antiquities, British Museum.

mother influence. The powers, gods, or deities which were worshipped in the temples were conceived to transcend the earth, and therefore, by contrast, were *positive* in nature or spirit. "Ra" was one of the most celebrated masculine creative powers. He reached down to earth and impregnated it with life. "Ra" was frequently depicted as a solar disc or circle. Thus we have in these two symbols, the *oblong* and the *circle,* a lesson in the creation of earth and creation of life by the combining of dual forces. We might say that one represented one polarity, and the other another.

Those who possessed such knowledge were under great oath not to reveal it wrongly, and would suffer dire consequences if they misused the *secret wisdom.* In a translation from the original hieroglyphic inscriptions in *The Book of the Dead,* by Sir E. A. Wallis Budge, we find these admonishments, "to allow no one to see it," nor was it to be recited to even a close friend, for further we find: "never let the ignorant person, or anyone whatsoever look upon it"; also "the things which are done secretly in the hall of the tomb are the *mysteries . . .*"

In some cases, classes of a very select nature were held in the private chambers of the reigning Pharaoh.

The members of such assemblies became more and more select, the teachings more profound, and the discussions so dialectic that there arose a most autocratic and secret society of the truly great minds of the day. Thus was laid the foundation of the Great White Brotherhood.

The first Pharaoh who conducted the class in his private chambers was Ahmose I, who reigned from 1580 B. C. to 1557 B. C. Because he was capable of conducting the great school as well as ruling the people with more civilized and advanced principles (due to his training in the school, no doubt), he is referred to as the "deliverer of Egypt" by some historians.

He was succeeded as Pharaoh by Amenhotep I, who became a teacher in the secret school for three years.

On January 12 (approximately), 1538 B. C., Thutmose I was crowned succeeding Amenhotep I. He owed his position to his wife, Ahmose, who was the first woman to become a member of the class on equal terms with the men. The discussion regarding her admittance (preserved in the Rosicrucian Archives) forms an interesting story and reveals the origin of some of the doctrines of the equality of the sexes.

Thutmose I was succeeded by Hatshepsut, his daughter, who ruled as a "king" independently and as co-regent with her half-brother Thutmose II, a son of Thutmose I by his marriage to Isis.

It was Thutmose III who organized the present physical form followed by the present secret Brotherhood and outlined many of its rules and regulations. He ruled from approximately 1500 B. C. until 1447 B. C., and his reign is unimportant to us except for his establishment of the Brotherhood.

History relates a very strange occurrence, in the life of Thutmose III, that is mystically important to us. We are told of a great feast which, oddly enough, if that is the term to use, occurred about on the occasion of the Spring equinox. This great festival was being held in the Temple of Amen, one of the prevailing gods of the time, in the great Temple of what is now Karnak at Thebes, Egypt, the then great capital city. We can visualize this ceremony, if we will; the magnificent colonnaded halls of this splendid edifice, the balmy air of a March evening in Egypt, the Nile nearby, swaying palm trees, the heavy shadows, the flickering light of the torches, the colorful attire of the priests and the assembly, the chanting, the soft strains of the string instruments.

Thutmose III, as was his custom, was present at the feast. He, with his colleagues, was seated in the Northern Hall of the great Temple. The chief priests or Kheri Hebs were perambulating and carrying a little image symbolic of the god Amen. As they passed the different groups of personages they were acclaimed. But, strangely, the High Priest would walk over to each group and peer into their faces as though he were searching for someone, and then as if realizing that they were not the ones, he would shake his head in the negative, and cross over to the opposite side and repeat the process. He knew all the time that Thutmose III was present, but finally when he reached the Northern Chamber of the Temple, he acted as though he had suddenly discovered the one for whom he had been searching. He placed at the feet of Thutmose III the image of Amen which depicted, in the customs of the time, that he, Thutmose III, had been chosen instead of his brother to succeed the father upon the throne, and the great assemblage broke forth in acclamation.

What interests us mostly, and which is recorded in history, is Thutmose III's explanation of his experience upon the occasion. He had no knowledge that he was to be chosen to become Pharaoh, because by right of accession, his brother should have been. But when the image was placed at his feet, he was seen to stand up; however, according to Thutmose III he felt "raised" as though his feet hardly touched the ground, and as though he had ascended into the heavens, and there he tells us God duly appointed him to serve his people. In fact, he felt as though he had been divinely ordained because of the mystical experience, and it became not even necessary for him to journey to Heliopolis where the Sun Temple was located, as had been the custom, to be formally coronated.*

He appears to have been quite original in his application of the doctrines of mysticism, but held to the existing external form of religion, possibly because of political conditions. Egypt was not free from the danger of the "grasping hand" of adjoining nations and the life of this ruler was constantly tormented by outbreaks of war; the cooperation of his military forces depended considerably upon his permitting the populace to indulge in all its fanciful beliefs—especially the idolatrous religions. For this reason an immediate change in the fundamentals of their religion—such as was made by Thutmose's descendant, Amenhotep IV, in 1355 with such reac-

---

*Breasted, *History of Egypt*. Chap. XV, p. 268.

tionary results—did not seem advisable or even necessary.

A gradual development in the existing mystical beliefs could be more easily and permanently accomplished by establishing a secret school of philosophy, the students of which would put into practice the high standards selected.

As in all ages there were those who might be called *advanced thinkers,* true philosophers, sages, and scholars. Many of these were students of the mystical doctrines as taught by Thutmose's predecessors, and they evidently had great faith in the final success of the principles; for when Thutmose proposed that the "class" which had been meeting in his chambers become a closed and secret order, "there was no dissenting voice, and articles of limitations were established ere the assembly dispersed in the early hours of dawn."

This grand "Council Meeting," for such it is considered in all official records of the Order, occurred during what would be the week of March 28th to April 4th of 1489 B. C., according to our present calendar. It is generally conceded to have been on Thursday, April 1st, but this may be associated with *Maunday Thursday,* a later establishment. However, Thursday has become the usual day for Rosicrucian meetings, and "Maunday" Thursday has become the occasion for special Temple Convocations in many AMORC Lodges of the world.

Twelve known Fratres and Sorores were present at this first Supreme Council. The Sorores were the wife of Thutmose III, known in the Order as *Mene;* the wife of one of the Fratres; and another who was a descendant of one of the rulers of a preceding dynasty. Therefore, there were nine Fratres and three Sorores at this Council, a combination of numbers very significant.

No worldly name was decided upon for the Brotherhood, the records showing that the predominating thought was the maintenance of secrecy.* The organization had no publicity; it required no propaganda other than personal advice to those whose presence was desired, and as the one word, translated into *Brotherhood* (a secret, fraternal body), was sufficient name for all purposes, we do not find any other term. This accounts for the widespread diversity of the name as adopted later. In many of the documents issued to the Grand Lodges throughout the entire world, the name of the Order is seldom mentioned.

---

*It must not be construed that the word *Rosicrucian,* or any variation of it, was used by, or applied to, this ancient brotherhood. This Egyptian Brotherhood was *not* Rosicrucian as we know the Order today, but rather the Order has its traditional roots in the ancient brotherhood. It derives its principles and objectives from it.

The idea of secrecy is so strong and predominant that the Order is referred to indirectly and sometimes erroneously (or perhaps diplomatically) as *it*, the *school*, the *brotherhood*, or the *council*. Furthermore many of these documents begin with the announcement: *"I, Brother of the Illuminati, with power decreed, do declare this Manifesto,"* or with the Salutation: "I, F. Illuminati of the 12." (I, Frater Illuminati of the 12th degree.) Very often these official manifestoes are signed: "With Peace Profound" and sometimes "F, Profundis" or "F, 12."

These words not only show that the twelfth or last degree has been the last circle within the Order, and known as the *Illuminati*, even to this day, but they also explain why some references are made to these documents as "Instructions of the Illuminati," which may easily be misinterpreted as "Instructions to the Illuminati" as one sees them referred to in works published abroad in the 15th, 16th, and 17th centuries A. D., where the *Order Rosae Crucis* is designated solely by the term *Illuminati*.

Furthermore, if one considers for a moment the prejudice—even the prohibition—against such secret Orders, one will appreciate the very evident attempts at subterfuge. Not only did certain bigoted religious organizations condemn all secret orders as "works of the devil," but those orders or schools which claimed to have *rare knowledge* of the sciences were severely criticised by the various scientific bodies of the day. As soon as learning became so general that competition arose between schools and students, the secret orders were widely condemned even though many of the most unfair critics of some were oath-bound members of others.

Though the Order had no definite name, Thutmose saw that it had very definite principles, rules, and modes of procedure, all of which have come down to us today without material change.*

At the close of his reign in 1447 there were thirty-nine Fratres and Sorores in the Council, and the meetings, which had become regular and systematic, were held in a hall of the Temple at Karnak, outside of which Thutmose III erected two obelisks bearing a record of his achievements.

Thutmose signed most of the decrees of the Council with his own *cartouche* and it became the Seal of the Order "in testimony of the great work of our teacher (Master) to be forever a mark of honor and loyalty." As was customary with these rulers when any event of national importance occurred,

---

*It is understood, therefore, that the present name of the Order was not used during the formative period of the Egyptian mystery schools.

Thutmose issued a *scarab* bearing his *cartouche* on one side, plus a mark which has a special meaning to all mystics. One original scarab, which was used for hundreds of years in Egypt by various officials to impress the Seal of the mystic fraternity in wax on all official documents, was given to the Grand Lodge of America with other jewels and papers of an official nature. It is considered one of the rarest antiquities of Egypt now in this country.

The Order here is to be congratulated on having in its possession one of the *oldest*, if not the most *sacred*, of all mystic jewels, one which has never been used by other than the Masters in Egypt. It means virtually the passing of the Master's Spirit from Egypt to America, as was planned by the founders centuries ago.

This Seal appears on the official documents of the Order of the present International Jurisdiction together with the American R. C. Seal, and its illegitimate use constitutes a forgery, according to the By-Laws of the Order throughout the world, punishable by a special decree of the Masters.

In this connection it may be explained that the Obelisk now in Central Park, New York City—one of the two erected in Egypt by Thutmose III and intended to stand some day in "the country where the Eagle spreads its wings"—bears this Cartouche, or Seal, as well as many other authentic and instructive signs now used by all Rosicrucians of the true Order. In Egypt today, the Rosicrucian Order, descending from very ancient lodges, uses this Cartouche as its official emblem above all others.

Before his transition, Thutmose III made his son (by Hatshepsut) co-regent. Thus Amenhotep II took up his father's work in the Brotherhood about the end of September, 1448 B.C. In the month of March—the seventeenth to be exact—1447 B.C., Thutmose passed to the Great Beyond, having been king (pharaoh) for nearly 54 years and being but one week less than 89 years of age. His mummy was found in the Cachette at Deir el-Bahri, and history acclaims him "the greatest pharaoh in the New Empire if not in all Egyptian history."

Amenhotep II ruled from 1448 to 1420 B.C. and he in turn was succeeded by his son Thutmose IV, who ruled from 1420 to 1411 B.C. Amenhotep III, son of the preceding, occupied the throne from 1411 to 1375 B.C. and was the last of the truly powerful pharaohs or emperors.

Upon the transition of Amenhotep III the Empire fell to his son Amenhotep IV, with whose history all

Rosicrucians are greatly concerned. He was the last Great Master in the family of the founders and the one to whom we owe the really wonderful philosophies and writings used so universally in all Lodge work throughout the world.

Amenhotep IV was born in the Royal Palace at Thebes, November 24th, 1378 B.C. His mother Tiy or Tia was of Aryan birth, but both he and his father paid the most sincere respects to her and were ever proud of designating her *Queen Tia* upon all monuments.

He was only eleven years old in 1367 B.C. when he was crowned and immediately began a career unequaled by any pharaoh of Egypt.

His father, having been the Master of the Order for a number of years, built the great Temple of Luxor and dedicated it to the Brotherhood. He also added to the Temple of Karnak and in many ways left "monuments of testimony and praise."

The Brotherhood numbered two hundred and eighty-three Fratres and sixty-two Sorores at this time, and at the time of the crowning of young Amenhotep IV, the Master was one Thehopset who remained in the office until 1365 B.C. Amenhotep's installation as *Master-by-Council-Decree* occurred in the Temple of Luxor, April 9th, 1365, at sunset, in the presence of his bride and her parents.

Amenhotep being the only descendant, it was deemed advisable that he marry as early as the customs then permitted in order that an heir to the throne would be assured. But Amenhotep's children unfortunately were daughters, and this proved disastrous to the throne.

The life of this great man is too easily found in various histories of Egypt, especially Breasted's, to warrant space here, but his accomplishments for the Order must be considered, at least briefly.

Since he was born in a country where people were given to idolatry, where the chief endeavors were those of building Temples to gods, it is easy to appreciate his attitude toward the existing religion (or religions) after he had been thoroughly instructed in the secret philosophy. So keen was his understanding that in his fifteenth year he composed many of the most beautiful prayers, psalms, and chants used in the organization today, as well as contributing to the philosophy and sciences.

To him came the inspiration of overthrowing the worship of idols and substituting the religion and worship of one God, a supreme deity, whose spirit was in Heaven and whose physical manifestation was the Sun—the *Symbol of Life.* This was in accordance with the secret doctrines, and it changed the worship of the Sun as a *god* to the worship of *the God* symbolized by the sun. This was the beginning of monotheism in Egypt and the origin of the worship of a spiritual deity which *"existed everywhere, in everything,* but was *nothing of the earth"* i.e., had no physical existence on earth in the form of inanimate or nonspiritual images.

Arthur E. P. Weigall, Chief Inspector of the Department of Antiquities, Upper Egypt, in writing of the religion inspired by Amenhotep IV (Akhnaton), says: "Like a flash of blinding light in the night time, the Aton (the sun-symbol of the true God) stands out for a moment amidst the black Egyptian darkness, and disappears once more—the first signal to this world of the future religion of the West. . . . One might believe that Almighty God had for a moment revealed himself to Egypt. . . ."

We shall let a portion of one of a number of hymns written by Amenhotep, and sung to the glory of the sole God, speak for itself:

How manifold are thy works!
They are hidden before men
O sole God, beside whom there
is no other.
Thou didst create the earth
*according to thy heart.**

Truly the religion of Amenhotep did not endure for long. Compared to the years of darkness, it was but a flash, for it ceased as a *public* and *general* religion when Amenhotep passed beyond the veil in 1350 B. C.

He, too, left many monuments to the glory of the Brotherhood. First, he removed as far as possible all "pillars to Ammon" and all references to Ammon as a *god*. So thorough was his work that he did not hesitate to mutilate the work done by his father, at Karnak and Luxor, by effacing all reference to the god Ammon—put there to appease the heathen priesthood—even to removing the name of his father and mother where they were connected with such idolatry. This naturally provoked the populace, especially since Amenhotep substituted beautiful monuments to the "living God."

---

*The word *heart* may mean either *pleasure* or *understanding* here. Compare this with Psalm 104:24, to see influence on early Hebrew Psalmist.

In the fifth year of his reign—when he was only sixteen years of age—a sweeping reform was initiated throughout Egypt by his decree, which prohibited any other form of worship except that already mentioned. In one of his decrees he wrote: "This is my oath of Truth which it is my desire to pronounce, and of which I will not say: 'It is false,' eternally forever."

He then changed his own name so that it would not be inconsistent with his reform. Amenhotep meant "Ammon is satisfied"; this he altered to Akhnaton or Ikhenaton meaning "pious to Aton" or "Glory to Aton."

He built a new capital at El Amarna (Akhetaton) in the plain of Hermopolis on a virgin site at the edge of the desert and abandoned Thebes because it was the *magnificent city of Ammon.* At El Amarna he also built a large Temple for the Brotherhood, in "the form of a cross," and a large number of houses for his Council. Here was the beginning of monastic life, for within the boundaries of El Amarna lived two hundred and ninety-six Fratres of the Order, each having taken an oath never to pass "beyond the shadow of the Temple."

These Fratres wore special costumes which included a "cord at the loins" and a covering for the head, while the priest in the Temple wore a surplice of linen and had his head shaved in a round spot on the top.

It is from this institution that all monastic orders, especially that of St. Francis, derive their methods, even their costumes.

During these years at El Amarna the Brotherhood was being made into a concrete organization, and the Fratres at this community outlined the initiations and forms of service as used today.

Akhnaton (Amenhotep IV) not only built his Temple in the form of a cross, but he added the cross and the rose as symbols and further adopted the Crux Ansata,* in a special coloring, as the symbol to be worn by all teachers (Masters). In fact, the last year of his life was spent in evolving a wonderful system of symbols used to this day, to express every phase and meaning of the Rosicrucian sciences, arts, and philosophies, and while some of these have become known to the uninitiated through the researches of Egyptologists, many remain secret and all are understandable only to the initiated.**

---

*The crux ansata is one of the earliest forms of a cross. It is an oval resting on a tau cross, or letter T. It was a symbol of life.

**The sciences and arts at the time, or the rituals, were not known as Rosicrucian. They descended to subsequently become a part of the present Rosicrucian traditions and rites.

As a ruler, our Master failed to check the desire for war. He foresaw the result of the approaching crisis and, sad at his neglect of political matters in his enthusiasm for the spiritual, he weakened his health and was finally forced to take to his bed in the month of July, 1350 B.C. Instead of using his mighty knowledge to regain his health it appears from his last dictated writings that his constant wish was to be spiritualized, that he might be *raised up to that plane* from which God's symbol shone down upon him. He fasted—practically starving himself—refused the services of the physician in the Order, and prayed constantly. Then, on July 24, late in the afternoon, with his right hand upstretched to God pleading to be taken into the *nous* he was seen by his Fratres and Sorores of the Order watching there, to be actually raised for a moment and then to drop back in "sweet repose with a smile of illumination upon his countenance."

Thus, passed to the beyond our Great Master, who did so much and left so much for our organization.

He may have neglected Egypt politically, but she will always remember her young Pharaoh whose twenty-eight years left her art and architecture, her sciences and philosophies so greatly changed and improved. His reign was like unto the Renaissance of France, and even the hieroglyphics and arts show a vast improvement based upon the principles of Truth. At the time of his crowning he took the title of "Amenhotep, King, *Living in Truth*," which was the Rosicrucian phrase of fidelity as it is today, and he passed onward to the other life in *truth*.

Perhaps the most summary of all testimonies to Amenhotep IV found outside of the Rosicrucian literature, is that paid by James Breasted, Professor of Egyptology, University of Chicago, who says in his *History of Egypt*: "The modern world has yet adequately to value, or even acquaint itself with this man, who in an age so remote and under conditions so adverse, became the world's first individual."

CHAPTER II

THE GROWTH OF THE ORDER
IN THE ORIENT

———

AT THE close of the first epoch of the Brotherhood's history, ending with the transition of Amenhotep IV (Akhnaton) in 1350 B.C., there was but one secret assembly, that which met in the Temple at El Amarna; and the Fratres and Sorores numbered four hundred and ten, including the Officers of the Lodge and the members of the Supreme High Council.

Plans had been made for years for the establishment of other assemblies or Lodges in various countries; but in those countries where a Lodge could have been established by one of the Egyptians who would have traveled there, war was raging and conditions were against any such institution.

Greeks were coming to Egypt to study its philosophies and become acquainted with its learning. Many of them sought entrance into the Order but it appears from various Council decisions that they were not admitted because of unpreparedness.

Benedictus Figulus, a Brother of the Order, who made a very exhaustive study of the growth of the Order, wrote: "About the year 1680 A.M.[1] the Greeks went to Chaldea and Egypt to learn this philosophy—but after learning a little they became so puffed up and proud, depending more than was meet on their own understanding."[2] This seems to have been the result most feared by the Council there, just as it is today. So many are ready to grasp at the first principles and then thinking their minds capable of building a philosophical structure upon the foundation, cease to be students and at once become teachers, each having a distinct, incomplete, and erroneous philosophy or "ism." Naturally there will be heretics in every school of thought; but a heretic is one who diverges from the established teachings only because of a *thorough knowledge* of such teachings, and to such we may turn for helpful criticism and suggestions at times. We must be delivered from the bigoted student who rises above his fellows and places his "superior" mind and judgment above the experienced understanding of his teachers.

---

[1] A. M. (year of the world—supposedly beginning at 4004 B. C.)
[2] "Dedicatory Speech to the Golden and Blessed Casket of Nature's Marvels," by Benedictus Figulus—p. 12. James Elliott and Company, London 1893.

For many years the Order progressed but little. Amenhotep IV left the work in the hands of competent teachers, and as the years passed by a few were admitted and initiated while the great teachings were being transcribed into symbolism and a special secret alphabet.

There being no male descendants of Amenhotep IV, he was succeeded by his son-in-law as Pharaoh, and at the close of the XVIII dynasty the religion of Ammon had been established once again, while the dreams and hopes of our Master were confined to the Order and its succession of teachers.

During the XIX dynasty under Seti I and Rameses II considerable tolerance was granted to the Order in Egypt; but gradually a feeling arose against its "secret power" and the lines of activity had to be drawn closer and closer.

Fortunately, in the Order at the time of the transition of Amenhotep IV, there was a sage named Hermes. So great was his learning and yet so mystical his many writings, purposely veiled so that they might be of value only to the future initiates, that the uninitiated minds of future years arose and acclaimed Hermes a myth, and there are those today who try to establish his identity with that of the Egyptian god "Thoth." However, it is the author's pleasure to state now that which has never appeared in print before, and which has perplexed investigators for centuries—the birth date of Hermes Trismegistus—the Thrice Great Man.* He was born in Thebes, October 9th, 1399 B.C. He lived to the age of one hundred and forty-two years, dying in the Rosicrucian Monastery at El Amarna, on March 22nd, 1257 B.C., and his mummy lies among others in a cachette in the vicinity of El Amarna.

He was "thrice great" because he lived to attend the installation of Amenhotep IV as an R. C. Master, became Master himself upon the latter's transition, and in 1259 installed one Atonamen as Master of the Order.

It was at this time that Hermes completed his writings, especially the seven books and tablets which were found and brought to light in 400 A.D., and which were upon diverse chemical and physical subjects.

The following quotation from the text, *Poemandres, the Shepherd of Men,* is a Greek version of the ancient writings of Hermes, relating a cosmological vision which he had. Though the wording may

---

*Dr. Budge, eminent Egyptologist, says that the Egyptians often referred to Hermes as "Lord of Maat," i. e., Lord of Truth, and that he was regarded as the inventor of all arts and sciences. "Lord of Books" is still another title assigned him.

have been actually influenced by Greek philosophical thought, it does show the attempt to preserve not only the name but the wisdom attributed to this great man:

"But in a little while darkness came settling down in part, awesome and gloomy, coiling in sinuous folds so that methought it like unto a snake.

"And then the darkness changed into some sort of a moist nature, tossed about beyond all power of words, belching out smoke as from a fire and groaning forth a wailing sound that beggars all description.

"(and) after that an outcry inarticulate came forth from it, as though it were a voice of fire.

"(Thereon) out of the light—a holy word (Logos) descended on that nature. And upwards to the height from the moist nature leapt forth pure fire; light was it, swift and active too. The air, too, being light, followed after the fire; from out of the Earth-and-Water rising up to fire so that it seemed to hang therefrom.

"But Earth-and-Water stayed so mingled each with other, that Earth from Water no one could discern. Yet were they moved to hear by reason of the Spirit-Word (Logos) pervading them."

In 1203 several of the Fratres of the Order who

were of the *Illuminati* were commissioned to go into other lands and spread the secret doctrines by the establishment of other Lodges. It was quite apparent that Egypt was to be subjected to a devastation and that its great learning might be lost. Confidence seems to have been the keynote, however, for one may read a long argument, reminding one of a speech in Congress, delivered by one of the Fratres at a Council held in El Amarna on June 8, 1202 B.C., in which he reassures all present that the "stars shew naught but trial, and test, by air, fire, and water, which we hold to be the elements of the crucible from which the precious stone will bring forth its own." And again: "who among us will rise and predict defeat for that which our Masters have labored over 29 cycles (two hundred years)? Is not this *Truth?* Are we not assembled in *Truth?* Are we not living *Truth?* And, can *Maat* ever die?* Is not transition the gateway of progress? And can the crucible do more than bring about a physical and spiritual transition, a transmutation, of the principles for which we have pledged our lives?"

---

*As early as 3500 B. C., the word *Maat* appeared as the epitome of those values of the moral order which men conceived, such as *truth, justice,* and *righteousness.* Later the chief justices of the Egyptian courts, we are informed by Dr. James Henry Breasted, wore Lapis Lazuli emblems upon their breasts, symbolizing *Maat.*

It was finally decided that "no undue haste should be sanctioned in permitting the Fratres who have gone abroad to establish Lodges, but rather that those who travel here in search of the Light should be tried, and to those found qualified shall be given the commission to return to their people and establish a Lodge in the name of the Brotherhood."

It was this dictum—known as the *AMRA*—that in later years proved the wisdom of the Councilors at this meeting, for it not only became a hard and fast rule, but made for the success of the plans of propagation.

It was in this wise that the phrase "travel East for learning or Light" first came into use; for those who soon began to travel to Egypt came from the West.

About the year 1000 B.C. there came to Egypt a character whose name is recorded as Saloman but who was identified in later years with Solomon.

The records show that he had come from the *West*, had traveled over many lands and across waters. He was of a nation which was large and important, situated in some very distant land. All this is indicated from the report he made to the representatives of the fraternity whom he interviewed at Thebes "whither he had gone immediately upon his arrival in Egypt accompanied by his slaves (!) and his *najah* (a word unknown to the translators)."

He desired instruction in the higher Egyptian sciences and philosophy, and was directed to El Amarna with a letter of introduction from the *intendant* at Thebes. He reached El Amarna on the 4th day of June, 999, under the name of Saloman, *the youthful seeker.*

Saloman did not complete his studies, for it is reported that he left El Amarna "before the fourth examination." He left with his Fratres and Sorores a definite feeling of love, wisdom, and virtue, and all were grieved at his sudden but announced departure.

The next word of him is as a resident at the *royal home* in Bubastis in the Delta where Shishak I (or Sheshonk) had established himself. This was in the year 952 B.C., and Saloman is referred to as an instructor to the Pharaoh's son. This is probably a mistake in translation, for in another place he is referred to as advisor in political matters, and this seems more probable in the light of future developments. Whether he had been at this residence all the intervening years from 999 to 952 B.C. is not definitely established, but there is a record of his presence at Thebes in the year 980 when he visited some *games* in company with the *intendant* of Thebes, and a group of scholars with whom he seemed on the most intimate terms.

Saloman seems to have been greatly influenced in Thebes and Bubastis by the religion of Ammon and conceived a form of philosophical religion which was a mixture of the Rosicrucian monotheism and the Egyptian idolatry. To him the *sun* became more than the mere symbol of a God; it was the living vital spirit of God, and while not the God, it was God's ethereal body. This would indicate that Saloman conceived God as being (a) personal, rather than *impersonal* as the Rosicrucians taught, and (b) dual, body and spirit, Father and Holy Ghost.

When Shishak I secured Thebes he appointed his son priest in the religion of Ammon, and gave his daughter, Aye, to Saloman to wed. Then within a year or so Saloman departed for Palestine where he became a mighty power, and by a prearranged plan, permitted Shishak I to rule over his people. The history of Saloman or *Solomon* in Palestine is too well known to warrant any further comment except on one point.

Five years after Saloman began his rule in Palestine he completed a Temple there in which to house a "society" or brotherhood such as he had found at El Amarna. An examination of the plans and cross-section views of the so-called Saloman's Temple shows it to be not only typically Egyptian in architecture and decoration, but copied after the mystic Temple at El Amarna, even to the location of the Altar, with the exception that the side structures which made the original building a *cross* were eliminated in Saloman's plans.

Saloman had the assistance of two who had traveled in Egypt as architects and artists—Hu-ram-abi of Tyre and one Hiram Abif.

The Saloman brotherhood was closely watched by the fraternity in Egypt, which had removed its headquarters to Thebes again because of political changes and the warring invasions in the territory of El Amarna, which eventually reduced the entire community to ruins.

It was found that Saloman restricted his order to males and adapted a great many of the details of the Rosicrucian initiations and services. At first it was believed that he would apply to the Grand Lodge in Thebes for a charter and make his work a branch of the R. C., but it became apparent before the first assembly was held that he was not adhering to the

Rosicrucian philosophy, for he used the sun as the exclusive symbol of his order.

Of the growth of the Saloman brotherhood, as it was officially called in all ancient documents, one may read in all literature bearing upon Freemasonry. It has evolved into a semi-mystical, speculative, secret, fraternal order of power and great honor, gradually altering the principles laid down by Saloman, it is true, but doing so for the greater benefit of man.

The Greeks were now coming to Thebes to study, and it was at this time that the world-wide spread of the organization began.

Pythagoras is very often mentioned as one of the earliest Messiahs of the order, but in truth there were many who preceded him. Among the first to become worldly famous in the order was Solon, who became the first chaplain who was not an Egyptian. He entered the order in 618 B.C., and remained a true Messiah until his transition in 550 B.C., leaving for our use some of the most beautiful and inspiring prayers ever spoken by a yearning soul. His sagacity is also seen in the counsel he gave those who sought his advice. The following has been given us by Diogenes Laertius, in his biography of Solon:

"Put more trust in nobility of character than in an oath."

"Do not be rash to make friends, and, when once they are made, do not drop them."

"In giving advice seek to help, not to please, your friend."

"Learn to obey before you command."

Contemporary with him was Anaximander, who came from Miletus to study at Thebes preceding the coming of Pythagoras.

Pythagoras was born in Samos on November 26th, 582 B.C. He entered the Order at Thebes on the second of April, 531, and having passed through all the initiations and examinations he entered the Illuminati, October 16, 529, and left at once for Crotona (Krotono), Italy, with jewels and documents to found a Grand Lodge there. There were a few so-called secret cults in existence at that time in Italy, and when Pythagoras began to promulgate his plans and admitted that women might not only become members, but could hold office, he attracted the attention of the most advanced thinkers of the day. Theano, the wife of Pythagoras, was one of the principal officers for three years. The Grand Lodge eventually had 300 brothers and sisters and issued many charters for local lodges of the order throughout Italy.

From this time onward toward the Christian period, great minds from many countries journeyed Eastward and Westward and *Crossed the Threshold,* and having completed the work and studies, passed again into the world's darkness to spread the *light* as they interpreted it.

As a historical record and a guide to the student who delights in research and antiquarianism, there will be given the names of those who came to Thebes to study, became Masters of Rosicrucian Lodges in other lands, and during their lifetimes published at least one book, an official work, treating on the Rosicrucian philosophies or sciences.

Many of the books or manuscripts to be listed are still extant in the original, or translated, and quite a few of them are in America. A perusal of any one of them convinces one of the author's real knowledge and experience in Rosicrucianism.

CHAPTER III

THE WORK OF THE DISCIPLES

OUTER activities of the Great White Brotherhood, during the pre-Christian Era, were centered in a number of branches controlled by one group of supreme officers who constituted the Rosicrucian Fraternity of Brethren of the Rosy Cross. The Supreme Masters of the Great White Brotherhood withdrew from public activity and with a council of eminent advisors constituted the esoteric body known thereafter as the Great White Lodge.

The first spread of Rosicrucianism to the Western world was from the great seats of learning of ancient Egypt, namely, Tell el-Amarna, Thebes, Heliopolis, and Alexandria. The great masters, sages, or Kheri Hebs (high priests), who presided over the instruction, were initiates of the Great White Brotherhood. They authorized eminent scholars as disciples to go forth and disseminate the light under various organization names. Even those in authority, who were not initiates, acknowledged the greatness of the Secret Wisdom in the archives of the order, and appealed for its release to the worthy, as we shall

see. Philadelphus, the Ptolemy principally respon-
sible for the establishment of the first great university at Alexandria, Egypt, about 305 B.C., sought
in the beginning, it is believed, to create a center of eclectic philosophy. For this purpose, he
had the Athenian orator and statesman and his
personal friend, Demetrius, invite the great minds,
the philosophers of Greece, to teach or impart
their knowledge to Alexandrian students. It
was apparently the intention to classify such
knowledge and select that which, in the opinion of Philadelphus and his associates, merited
dissemination. The enthusiasm which the great
school inspired in the seeking minds of the
day altered the plans. The policy changed to research and advancement of knowledge, on the one
hand, and on the other hand, a careful preservation in the great library of all the wisdom of
all ages. Philadelphus became aware of the vast
knowledge of natural law and of a Cosmic philosophy had by those who were *initiates* of the mystery schools. Much of such knowledge seemed to
parallel that which he was having introduced
in Alexandria from the West—from Athens.
His consequent actions prove that he realized
that much of the Western knowledge was syn-
cretic, and had formerly come from Egypt. In

fact, Plato tells us that Solon got his information from the priests of Sais, who told him that all of the records were preserved in the Temple of Neith. A further tradition relates that Solon, Thales, and Plato all visited the great college at Heliopolis, and that the last mentioned studied there.

A contemporary of Philadelphus was Manetho, a High Priest at Heliopolis, and a learned man, also a prominent scribe of the Great White Brotherhood, who had access to the secret teachings of the Order. Manetho was also master of the ancient Egyptian writing, or Hieroglyphics, which, in the Third Century B.C., was becoming archaic and could not be generally read. The Egyptians were at that time reading a modern version of the ancient writings, the Demotic, and Greek was becoming still more popular. Philadelphus commissioned Manetho to compile a history of Egypt, and particularly a text of the *mystic philosophy* of the Secret Schools of the Great White Brotherhood and Rosicrucians. This knowledge, we are told, was mainly contained in the Hieroglyphic inscriptions in the library of the priesthood at Ra. It will be recalled that Amenhotep IV (Akhnaton) declared Ra, the sun, to be a physical manifestation or symbol of the great *sole God*. This library, therefore, must have contained the great truths of his monotheistic religion, and the truths which the thinkers with which he surrounded himself at Tell el-Amarna discovered. Much that we know of the outer or profane history of Egypt came about through this compilation by Manetho. In fact, it is generally conceded that Plutarch acquired much of his information from this source. In a book of Manetho's, called *Sothis,* of which fragments only are to be found in the writings of others, appears the following letter to Philadelphus, from Manetho, telling of his efforts to compile the ancient wisdom:

"We must make calculations concerning all the points which you may wish us to examine into, to answer your questions concerning what will happen to the world. According to your commands, the sacred books, written by our forefather, Thrice-greatest Hermes, which I study, shall be shown to you. My Lord and King, farewell."

Manetho's greatest work was his Egyptian history, which was done in three books, and in the Greek language. It is famous because it is the only work in Greek based upon a full knowledge of the Egyptian sources. Fragments of these works come to us today in the writings of Flavius Josephus and Julius Africanus. The former is a more reliable authority and refers to Manetho in his treatise, *Against Apion*. In the *History of Egypt* by Manetho, there is an interesting reference to Moses, which shows him also to have been an initiate of the Great White Brotherhood of Egypt, and to have transmitted their knowledge in a veiled manner to his people. The excerpt reads:

"Moses, a son of the tribe of Levi, educated in Egypt and initiated at Heliopolis, became a High Priest of the Brotherhood under the reign of the Pharaoh Amenhotep. He was elected by the Hebrews as their chief and he adapted to the ideas of his people the science and philosophy which he had obtained in the Egyptian mysteries; proofs of this are to be found in the symbols, in the Initiations, and in his precepts and commandments. The wonders which Moses narrates as having taken place upon the Mountain of Sinai, are, in part, a veiled account of the Egyptian initiation which he transmitted to his people when he established a branch of the Egyptian Brotherhood in his country, from which descended the Essenes. The dogma of an 'only God' which he taught was the Egyptian Brotherhood interpretation and teaching of the Pharaoh who established the first monotheistic religion known to man. The traditions he established in this manner were known completely to only a few of them, and were preserved in the *arcanae* of the secret societies, the *Therapeutics* of Egypt and the *Essenians.*"

Nearly five centuries later, during what might be said to be a period of decline of mysticism, or the mystic philosophy in the Western world, an emissary was sent from Egypt to Rome to capture the hearts and minds of the peoples, with a true mysticism free of the superstitions of the cults, and tempering the cold intellectualisms that were flourishing there. The world generally calls his great work *Neo-Platonism,* but it corresponds to the Rosicrucian doctrines of mysticism before as well as subsequent to his time. This master teacher was Plotinus. He was born in Lycopolis, Egypt, in 205 (?) A.D. For eleven years he was the personal student of Ammonius Saccas, at the great school at Alexandria. Ammonius Saccas related to him the doctrines of Plato, and he was instrumental in having Plotinus initiated into the inner circles of the Great White Brotherhood. He was carefully trained and prepared to introduce an aspect of the Platonic philosophy, with which the world was generally familiar, combined with the true mysticism and occult philosophy of the Secret Schools. This combination was necessary, for if he had attempted to present the latter in its true form during his time, it would have been rejected. By making it appear a new kind of Platonic teachings, people investigated it and were intrigued by the subtle beauty of these Eastern teachings.

Plotinus travelled extensively, as part of a military expedition in Persia, so that he could learn firsthand the Persian religion and philosophy. The influence of their beliefs is found in his dualism of good and evil as a single force, which is recognized in the mystical teachings of the Rosicrucians today. He entered Rome in 244 A.D., and founded his school as part of the great outer activity of the Great White Brotherhood. He was universally revered, not alone for his learning, but for his character. He was held in high respect by Emperor Gallienus and his consort Salonina.

Notable among the phases of the spread of the work of the Rosicrucians to other lands was the establishment of two branches known as the *Essenes* and the *Therapeuti*. The Essenes constituted that branch which went into Palestine and adopted a distinct name in order to veil its preliminary work while the Therapeuti was a similar branch established for the same purpose in Greece.

In Palestine the Essenes established a community of members and associate members at Galilee where they had many homes in this non-Jewish, Gentile part of the country, and built their principal monastery and temple on the top of Mount Carmel where Elijah, as one of the descendants of the Great White Brotherhood, had previously established a retreat and had taught many of the mysteries of the Brotherhood.

Just before the Christian period, the Great White Brotherhood had also established a new monastery and temple and other structures for a great central point of their activities at Heliopolis, and the temple here was known as the Temple of Helios, or sometimes called "the Temple of the Sun." The intercourse between the temple at Heliopolis and the one on top of Mount Carmel was intimate and frequent, and many of the philosophers who journeyed from European points to Egypt to study spent some of their time at Mount Carmel.

Just about the time of the birth of Jesus the great library and archivist records maintained at Heliopolis were transferred to Mount Carmel, and the Essene Brotherhood in Palestine together with other branches of the Great White Brotherhood were preparing for the coming of the great Avatar who was to be the reincarnation of Zoroaster, a famous Avatar of the Brotherhood in centuries past.

The birth of Jesus in a family of Gentiles living in the Essene community at Galilee fulfilled the expectations of the Brotherhood, and from this time on the outer and inner activities of the Brotherhood became centered around the ministry of the great Master Jesus. The details of the birth, preparation, ministry, and culminating events of the Master Jesus are all set forth in a separate volume entitled *The Mystical Life of Jesus* wherein are given details from the records of the Essenes and the Great White Brotherhood and which have never been published before.* Therefore, I will not take space in the present record to recite these many and important matters.

At the close of the life of Jesus the Christ, the disciples of Jesus and the high officers of the Great White Brotherhood planned to carry on the new cycle of illumination and revelation of doctrines as presented by him, and an outer congregation or public movement was established known as the Christine Church. This movement gradually evolved into a more or less independent public organization. While it was sponsored by the Great White Brotherhood, and all of the principal workers like unto the

---

The Mystical Life of Jesus, by H. Spencer Lewis, Ph.D.

[83]

original Apostles were men chosen from the Essene Gentile community at Galilee, the Great White Brotherhood did not establish the Christine Church as a part of its activities, because it was interested in the work of all religious movements in all lands, and did not become a part of any of them.

Several hundred years after the foundation of the Christine Church, and while it was being actively promulgated by the representatives of the Great White Brotherhood in those lands where the doctrines and teachings would do the utmost good, the Supreme Temple and monastery, as well as the library and archivist records, were transferred from Mount Carmel to new structures built in an isolated section of Tibet where the Headquarters of the Great Masters of the organization was maintained for some time.

During the time of the organization of the Christine movement, and throughout all the centuries thereafter, the inner circle of the Great White Brotherhood continued to function as a nonsectarian, nonreligious school of mystical, occult, and scientific teachings. All of the outer activities such as the Essene movement, the Christine movement, and similar bodies in various lands, represented the outer congregation of the Great White Brotherhood while the secret schools and temples with their high priests and instructors and large membership of students represented the inner congregation. All through the ages up to the present time the Great White Brotherhood has continued to function in this dual manner.

It was during the period of contentions and strife which the Christine movement faced, that the Great White Brotherhood found it advisable to establish another organization composed almost exclusively of men, and called the *Militia Crucifera Evangelica*. Its purpose was to protect the cross as a mystical symbol, against its misuse by those who attempted to carry on crusades of persecution against others who would not accept a sectarian interpretation of the symbolism of the ancient emblem. It was in the foundation of this Militia that we find the origin of all the militant organizations which became defenders of the faith in later years. It is notable, however, that the Militia Crucifera Evangelica never became an active body of prosecutors or crusaders, but merely of silent defenders who were pledged never to unsheathe the sword except in absolute defense. The organization became greatly enlarged in later centuries, not as a true military organization, but as a group of those who defend the Rosicrucian emblem and the cross with their moral strength rather than with any physical strength.

The Militia Crucifera Evangelica continues today throughout the world as a small but courageous and active body perpetuating its traditional ideals. In July of 1940, the members of the American jurisdiction, authoritatively established by European decree, met in San Jose, California, in their first *official* conclave for the Western world. The principal purpose of the convention was the adoption of a means to defend Christianity and mystical concepts at a time when humanity was again afflicted by a second World War.

Throughout the centuries preceding the Christian Era and thereafter, the Great White Brotherhood and its centers of learning, its libraries and monasteries, became the centers for pilgrimages on the part of great minds seeking illumination and the highest advancement in culture and ethics. The records of the Brotherhood are replete with the life stories of many eminent characters known in general history who became students in the mystery temples of the organization in Egypt, at Palestine, or elsewhere. They later presented outlines of modified philosophies and principles which the public could understand and apply, and became authors of books which have been valuable contributions to the advancement of learning.

Among the very earliest of the philosophers who contributed to the Rosicrucian philosophy were: the fellow workers of Hermes—Mena, Busiris, Simandius, Sesostris, Miris, Sethon, Amasis, Adfar Alexandrinus, and King Calid.

Then there was "Maria Hebraeae," a Hebrew woman supposed to have been Miriam, a sister of Moses.

After the journey of Pythagoras to Italy many came from Greece and other lands to be initiated in Egypt and from there returned to their native lands or elsewhere to establish branches of the mystic school and become Masters and Officers therein.

Most of these—whose names are listed below, published during their lifetimes one or more papers dealing with various principles of the Rosicrucian philosophy and science.

Some of these writings were kept secret—others were written for public reading with the true doctrines carefully veiled. In order that the Rosicrucian students may study such writings as are extant today these philosophers' names are given and sometimes the name or title of their work which is especially recommended.

Solon, c. 639-c. 559 B.C.

Anaximander of Miletus, 611-547 B.C.

Anaximenes of Miletus, 520 B.C.

Heraclitus of Ephesus, 520 B.C.

Parmenides, 515 B.C.

Empedocles of Agrigentum, 500 B.C.

Democritus of Thrace, 460 B.C.

Socrates of Athens, 470?-399 B.C.

Euclides of Megara, 450?-374 B.C.

Plato of Athens, 427?-347 B.C.

Aristotle of Thrace, 384-322 B.C. (Read *De Anima* and the *Metaphysica.*)

Epicurus of Athens, 342?-270 B.C.

Metrodorus, Hermarchus, Colotes, Leonteus and his wife Themista, and Leontium—all pupils of Epicurus in his R.C. Lodge in Athens, 306-301 B.C.

Philo of Alexandria, 110 B.C.

Antiochus of Ascalon, 100 B.C.

Cicero, 106-43 B.C.

Nigidius Figulus, 70 B.C.

Seneca, 54 B.C.?-A.D. 39

Plotinus, A.D. 205?-270

———

THE CHRISTIAN PERIOD

After these came philosophers from the Christian period beginning a new line of writers.

From this time on the work spread very rapidly throughout many lands and only a brief list of the most prominent can be given. The following not only contributed interesting writings to the future R.C. literature, but were either Masters of various Lodges or assisted in bringing the mystic fraternity into their respective countries.

Geber, or Jabir, Arab scholar, fl. 721-776. (*The Sum of Perfection*)

Charlemagne, king of the Franks, 742-814.

Al-Farabi, 870-950, compiler of encyclopedia of R.C. Science and Arts.

Avicenna of Bokhara, Persia, 980-1037.

Raymond VI, Count of Toulouse, defender of the Albigenses, 1156-1222.

Albertus Magnus, German scholastic, 1193?-1280. (*De Alchimia*)

Jean de Meung of France, 13th century. (*Roman de la Rose*)

Roger Bacon of England, 1214?-1294. (*Opus Majus*)

Thomas Aquinas, Italian theologian, 1225?-1274.

Arnold of Villanova of Catalonia, 1235?-?1312. (*Rosarium Philosophorum*)

Raymond Lully of Spain, 1235?-1315. (*Anima artis transmutationis* or *Clavicula*)

Dante Alighieri, 1265-1321. (*Divine Comedy*)

Nicholas Flamel of France, 1330?-1418. (*Exposition of the Hieroglyphical Figures*)

Thomas Norton, 15th century. (*Ordinall of Alchemy*)

Johannes Trithemius, 1462-1516.

Pico della Mirandola, Italian humanist, 1463-1494. (*Oration on the Dignity of Man*)

Cornelius Heinrich Agrippa, German physician, theologian, and writer, 1486?-1535. (*De occulta philosophia*)

Sir George Ripley, c. 1490. (*Twelve Gates*)

Paracelsus, Swiss alchemist and physician, 1493?-1541.

Dr. John Dee, English mathematician and astrologer, 1527-1608. (*Hieroglyphic Monad*)

Simon Studion, 1543-?1605. (*Naometria*)

Giordano Bruno, Italian philosopher, 1548?-1600. (*Concerning the cause, principle, and one*)

Johann Arndt, German theologian, 1555-1621. (*Zweytes Silentium Dei*)

Heinrich Khunrath, 1560-1605. He established the first R.C. library in Germany.

Sir Francis Bacon, past Imperator of the Order, 1561-1626. (*New Atlantis*)

Tommaso Campanella, Italian philosopher, 1568-1639.

Michael Maier, Grand Master of the R.C. Order in Germany, 1568-1622. (*Themis Aurea*)

Robert Fludd, English physician and Rosicrucian apologist, 1574-1637. (*Tractatus Apologeticus*)

Jacob Boehme, German theosophist and mystic, 1575-1624. (*Three Principles* and *Mysterium Magnum*)

Jean Baptiste van Helmont, Flemish physician and chemist, 1577-1644. (*De vita aeterna*)

Dr. William Harvey, 1578-1657.

Johann Valentin Andrea, 1586-1654.

Jan Amos Komensky (Comenius), Czech theologian and educator, 1592-1670.

René Descartes, French scientist and philosopher, 1596-1650. (*Discours de la Méthode* and *Meditationes de Prima Philosophia*)

Sir Robert Moray, 1600?-1673.

Benedictus Figulus, c.1608.

Elias Ashmole, 1617-1692. His collection of rarities, presented to Oxford, contained a manuscript copy of the *Fama Fraternitatis*.

Irenaeus Agnostus, c.1619. (*Portus Tranquillitatis*)

John Evelyn, 1620-1706.

Thomas Vaughan, a Welshman, who wrote under the name of Eugenius Philalethes, 1622-1665. He translated the early R.C. papers into English. (*Euphrates: or The Waters of the East* and *Lumen de Lumine*)

Jane Leade, English mystic, 1623-1704.

Dr. John Frederick Helvetius, 1625-1709. (*Golden Calf*)

Robert Boyle, British physicist, chemist, and natural philosopher, 1627-1691.

John Heydon, a Master in the English R.C. Order, 1629-1667. (*English Physitians Guide: or A Holy Guide*)

Baruch Spinoza, 1632-1677.

Sir Christopher Wren, English architect, 1632-1723. He designed and rebuilt St. Paul's Cathedral after the Great Fire in London of 1666.

Sir Isaac Newton, 1642-1727. An English natural philosopher and mathematician, who conceived the idea of universal gravitation set forth in his *Principia.*

Gottfried Wilhelm von Leibnitz, German philosopher and mathematician, 1646-1716. (*On the True Theologia Mystica*)

Johannes Kelpius, 1673-1708, Grand Master of the R.C. Order in its first cycle in America in 1694.

Dr. Christopher Witt, 1675-1765.

Conrad Beissel, 1690-1768.

Benjamin Franklin, 1706-1790. American statesman, scientist, and philosopher, he was associated with the Rosicrucians of Pennsylvania during the Order's first active cycle in America.

Peter Miller, 1710-1796.

Martínez de Pasquales, Portuguese mystic, 1715?-1779. He founded a society of mystics later led by Marquis Louis Claude de Saint-Martin.

Count Alessandro Cagliostro of Sicily, 1743-1795. Became a Master and established many R.C. lodges in Europe. (*Rituel de la Maçonnerie Egyptienne*)

Thomas Jefferson, 1743-1826. Statesman, scientist, philosopher, and third President of the U.S.

Louis Claude de Saint-Martin, 1743-1803. This French mystic and philosopher carried on the work of Martínez de Pasquales. His society became known as the Martinists.

Johann Wolfgang von Goethe, German poet and mystic, 1749-1832. (*Die Geheimnisse*)

[92]

John O'Donnell, 1749-1805.

Karl von Eckartshausen, 1752-1803. (*Cloud on the Sanctuary*)

William Blake, English artist, poet, and mystic, 1757-1827.

Dr. John Dalton, English chemist and physicist, who arranged the table of atomic weights, 1766-1844.

Marshal Michel Ney, 1769-?1815.

Michael Faraday, English chemist and physicist, 1791-1867.

Honoré de Balzac, French mystic and writer, 1799-1850. (*Louis Lambert*)

Edward George Bulwer-Lytton, English mystic and writer, 1803-1873. (*Zanoni*)

Eugene Sue, French novelist, 1804-1857. (*Wandering Jew*)

Giuseppe Mazzini, 1805-1872.

Anton Rubinstein, Russian Jewish pianist and composer, 1829-1894.

Dr. Franz Hartmann, 1839-1912.

Julius Friedrich Sachse, historian of the Rosicrucian movement in America, 1842-1910.

Ella Wheeler Wilcox, American poet, 1850-1919.

Elbert Hubbard, American writer, printer, and philosopher, 1856-1915.

Claude Debussy, French composer, 1862-1918.

Marie Corelli, English writer of mystical fiction, 1855-1924.

Nicholas Roerich, Russian-born mystic, artist, and philosopher, 1874-1947.

François Jollivet Castelot, d.1937.

△▽△

When the Rosicrucian movement reached what is now France, early in the Christian Era, it found there its greatest welcome.

The pilgrims to the Holy Land had brought back to the Counts and Lords of the South of France reports of the activities of a certain secret society devoted to science and brotherhood. Charlemagne was at the time conducting his great school of learning. History will tell the lay mind a great deal regarding his famous school. He realized that through education alone could he build his power and hold the reins of government. He gathered around him the brightest scholars of the day, the learned men of many countries, and offered them excellent remuneration if they would devote all their time to the teaching of the pupils in this school. The pupils included himself, his family, his relatives, and a few of his appointed officials.

Nor were these learned men limited to teaching. Charlemagne desired to promote learning. He gave his tutors every opportunity to make extensive researches in every field and provided them with an experimental laboratory. The philosophers—among them was the famous Alcuin—were permitted to travel to other lands to bring back the cream of all knowledge. In this school, St. Guillem, a nephew of Charlemagne, received his education.

One of these philosophers, Arnaud, was directed to go to Jerusalem in A.D. 778 to learn all he could about this wonderful secret society which possessed the key to all science and all art. Arnaud journeyed to Jerusalem and was there directed to Egypt. It is recorded that he made humble application for admission into the Order in Thebes, and then, in accordance with the Law AMRA, applied for permission to establish a branch Lodge in France [then the Frankish Empire].

Arnaud completed his study in Egypt in approximately two years and one month. Because of the difficulty of communication his several letters and reports to Charlemagne failed to reach their destination, and in France he was given up as dead—a fate which befell many who journeyed far in those days. One of his letters to Charlemagne, written on a papyrus in Thebes, was afterward found in a monastery near Millau in France, where it had been deposited in a vault among other rare papers for some unknown reason. In it Arnaud makes a very glowing report of his discoveries, and refers to the body of "silent students clothed in white as pure and spotless as their characters but diligent in their mastery of God's laws and privileges." In closing his report he says: "Should it be my privilege, my great honor, to bring to our land the seal and signs of this great school, we shall have in our midst the power which our beloved Master may use in destroying all ignorance, provided, of course, our Master shall deem it wise and beneficial to humble himself, not to those who ask it, but to God, and thereby become as one of the disciples of our Lord Jesus."

The significance of this closing sentence will be brought to mind when it is recalled that the religious feeling in Charlemagne's school was very intense and sincere. Bear in mind, Arnaud was trying to state diplomatically and respectfully that it would be necessary for Charlemagne to become a humble supplicant for admission into the Order if he wished to become a Master of the Order in France—a position and honor which Arnaud and his colleagues would certainly have insisted upon.

Arnaud returned to France in 802, however, and was given a very interesting ovation in the chamber of Charlemagne's throne. Charlemagne did not become a Master in the Order, but after two years' delay permitted a Lodge to be established in Toulouse. The original Lodge was founded in a temporary monastery on the outskirts of Tolosa—the ancient city—which is now in ruins some little distance from the present city of Toulouse. Part of the Altar of this first Lodge in France was still preserved by the archivists of the Order in France in 1909, though it was much the worse for very severe handling during the many religious wars in the Provinces.

Arnaud became the Master in that first Lodge which held its opening convocation about 804-805. (The difficulty with exact dates is due to the many changes in the calendar and in interpreting the various methods of keeping records in those days.)

The first Grand Master of France was Frees, who reigned from 883 to 899 A. D. Until that time Grand Masters were not appointed. There was to be only one Lodge in any country, according to the original plans, and the Master of that Lodge held no other power or authority than rule over the one Lodge. The granting of charters was still in the hands of the Supreme Council. But it was Frees who brought before the Council the advisability of establishing Grand Lodges in certain countries and giving to the Masters the right to grant charters to other Lodges within the same national confines. It was only one year before Frees passed to the beyond—898—that he received his authority and instructions to establish other Lodges in France and the second Lodge was immediately established in Lyons.

There were many devout students of the Order in Toulouse who lived in Lyons and they lost no time—after years of waiting—in getting a very flourishing Lodge established there. Many years later—1623—the Freemasons in Lyons organized a Rose Croix degree in the same city to please the many Rosicrucians who were Masons. The Masonic body was organized at a Council held there July 23rd, 1623.

In the meantime the Order in France had spread very rapidly and had attracted wide attention. Some of the Monks in the various monasteries in the South of France became interested, and without mentioning names at this time—let it be known that some of these Roman Catholic persons, devout and sincere, rendered a great service to the up-building of the sanctity of the Order by contributing many beautiful moral and spiritual creeds and dogmas.

Finally in 1001—the year when all the South of France was expecting the end of the world—according to an old Biblical prophecy—the Order in France established a Rosicrucian Monastery—the first in the world—in the old Roman city of Nemausus, now Nimes.

This Monastery became the nucleus for the great Rosicrucian College or Ecole R. C. which flourished in France from the twelfth century to the middle of the sixteenth and which was revived again in 1882 in Montpellier.

The history of the Order in France is very interesting. The most minute facts of the early history were recorded by Phonaire, who was the Official Historian of the Order in 1132 to 1134. The later history was compiled by a number of Masters of the R. C., R. F. and preserved in the archives in the Dongeon at Toulouse. This latter city has been the meeting place of the French Supreme Council since 1487. France held second place in strength of number of members, Germany holding first place, and England third. Egypt of course was the great Supreme Center, but had only a comparatively small number of members.

In France, the loss of membership through the great war was enormous.* Of the French Supreme Council of twenty-five, there were living in December of 1915 only seven. But the loss in Germany had been even greater. Many of the Brothers of the Or-

___

*This refers to the first World War.

der in France were called upon to bear arms; yet all did not reach the front, for some were classified and placed in offices and laboratories. Then, again, a great many of the French Brothers were older men, some of whom held high offices in the army, navy, and general government. Thus it was that all the Brothers of the Order in France did not participate in the actual conflict.

The Order spread into Germany shortly after the Grand Lodge was established in France. Charlemagne himself was the first to introduce the Order in Germany, for by his command one Mause settled somewhere along the Rhine near Coblenz and there began propaganda for members in a quiet dignified manner. He never lived to see his work bear fruit, however, for the restrictions placed around membership were severe and too stringent, but in 1100 a Lodge was established in Worms, and this became the Grand Lodge.

The work grew rapidly in Germany during the twelfth century, but it remained so secret and so inactive in its outward manifestations during its 108 years of inactivity that little was known of the Order or its members. Toward the beginning of the fifteenth century a spell of quietude—of dormancy —came again to the Order and as its members passed on few were admitted. Religious controversies and other troubles not of interest here threatened the complete destruction of the Order. At the beginning of the fifteenth century there were only about seven hundred Brothers and Sisters of the Order living within the jurisdiction of the German Grand Lodge at Leipzig.

But in the fifteenth century—at almost the last moment—the great revival came again. While this revival brought new life, new vigor and new hope to the Order in Germany, it has proved to be the most perplexing one that ever came to the Order anywhere throughout the world. It has left a question, a doubt, unanswered and unsettled, in the layman's mind and has caused more misunderstanding of the Order's true history and ancestry than this humble attempt by me will ever be able to make clear.

CHAPTER IV

THE 108-YEAR CYCLE AND "C.R-C."

———

IT IS necessary, just at this point in the history, to refer to one of the very mysterious and puzzling laws of the organization, the origin of which is lost in the traditional history, but the general acceptance of which accounts for many of the peculiar breaks in the activities of the organization.

It appears from many ancient writings that in the first centuries preceding the Christian Era the organization complied with a regulation which may have been established centuries before, or may have been tried at this time as a new regulation. This regulation called for a periodicity of active and inactive cycles, each of 108 years. The number of 108 is significant in itself to all occult students, but just why this new regulation was brought into effect is not known.

According to the terms of this regulation, every branch jurisdiction was to select a certain year as the anniversary of its original foundation, and from that year onward operate in accordance with the periodicity of cycles.

A complete cycle of existence from birth to rebirth was to be of 216 years. Of this cycle, the first 108 years was to be a period of outer, general activity, while the second period of 108 years was to be a period of concealed, silent activity, almost resembling complete dormancy. This period of inactivity was to be followed by another 108 years of outer activity, just as though a new Order of the organization was born without any connection with the previous cycles. This regulation seemed to be a close analogy to the cycles of birth and rebirth for the human family, except that the number of years in each cycle was different. Just as man's rebirth on earth was considered a reincarnation of his previous existence, so each new birth of the organization in each jurisdiction was to be considered the birth of a new organization as a reincarnated soul in a *new body*.

So we find in the first few centuries preceding the Christian Era the Order seemed suddenly to disappear from all outward existence and all outward activity in some of the older branches in the Orient. So far as the uninitiated were concerned, and so far as the casual historians recorded the events, the older branches forming a part of the foundation of the Rosicrucian Order suddenly ceased to exist without any explanation, or any indication that they would be revived. The members of the branches, and the great leaders, did not cease to carry on their *individual* activities, and we know from the records of the organization that, according to the rules and regulations regarding these periods of silence, during the 108 years of inactivity the members of the organization privately initiated their own descendants in their immediate families, but accepted no new members from the profane world. Thus several generations of Rosicrucians, initiated within the privacy of homes or secret temples, continued to carry the heritage of the Order in some lands, while outwardly and in all of its general activities the Order seemed to have gone out of existence. Then for several years preceding the time of the new birth, many prepared themselves by getting in contact with an active branch of the organization in other lands, and at the proper time announced in their own land the birth of a new cycle of the Order.

In most of the foreign lands the periods of dormancy and the periods of activity were not coincidental. Therefore, we find, for instance, that Germany was in the midst of a period of dormancy as far as the outer activities of the Order were concerned, during a time when the Order was very active in France and Holland. Again we find that the Order was inactive in France just at the time that the Order had its new birth in Germany, and the Order in England was in the very center of its period of activity.

The Mystery of C. R-C.

As the time approached for each jurisdiction or country to have its new birth of the Order, arrangements were made for the usual issuance of a manifesto or pamphlet setting forth the beginning of a new cycle. Just when this custom was adopted it is difficult to say, and of course in the early pre-Christian days, the issuance of pamphlets or printed matter was impossible, and so a decree was promulgated or disseminated by word of mouth and by the display of a certain symbol among the people. This manifesto, decree, or symbol, announced the opening of a "tomb" in which the "body" of a great master, C. R-C., was found, together with rare jewels and secret writings or engravings on stone or wood which empowered the discoverers of the "tomb" to establish the secret organization once again.

We will find later on in our history that when the time came for the new birth in Germany, the incident of the opening of the "tomb" was given wider circulation than had ever been given to a similar incident in any land before. This was due to the invention of the art of printing, which made possible the distribution of the manifestoes and the announcements in the form of pamphlets issued in five different languages, and disseminated through many nations at the same time. Coming at a crucial hour, as we shall see, in the evolution of religion and philosophy, and being so widely distributed, the pamphlets of the seventeenth century attracted such universal attention among persons who had never heard of the organization before that a common impression was created and recorded to the effect that a *new* organization, never known in the world before, had come into existence through the discovery of a tomb, and the body of a person unique in history. This false impression was recorded in so many later histories, that even today we are required to explain the misconception.

It must be apparent to the reader of this history that the discovery of a "body" in the "tomb," or the finding of the "body" of a person known as C. R-C., is allegorical, and is not to be taken in a literal sense. In the first place, the word "body" in the language in which it was first used, was symbolical of something entirely different than the *physical body* of a man. In the second place, the initials C. R-C., did not mean *Christian Rosenkreuz,* except as the words represented by those initials were translated in the *German* language. The initials C. R-C., standing for the *Christus* of the *Rosy Cross,* may be translated into the Latin, French, and other languages without any change; therefore the initials C. R-C., when first used were not the initials of either *German* or *French* words, but of Latin words.

Those writers of mystical and fantastical stories who have tried to present the story of C. R-C., by stating that these initials were those of an individual, are wholly unacquainted with the facts. Even if the spiritual person represented by the "body" of C. R-C., were the same in each cycle, through a series of reincarnations, such a reincarnated person would be a different *earthly individual* in each incarnation. For that reason it must be understood that there was no one earthly person who was *uniquely* and *exclusively* known as C. R-C., in any cycle of the Order's existence. Our records refer to at least twelve discoveries of "tombs" containing the "body" of C. R-C. in different lands preceding the greatly popularized incident in Cassel, Germany, in the seventeenth century. There have been similar incidents in the history of the Order since the one in the seventeenth century.

Therefore, when the student of the history of the organization finds the various breaks in the outer activities of the organization he soon notices that there is a periodicity to the breaks, and almost unconsciously sets down the dates of the cycles of activity and dormancy. We shall note a few of these dates as we proceed with the history in the different lands.

However, everyone who reads in some of the modern mystical books, and even in those that claim to be Rosicrucian, the story of "Christian Rosenkreuz" being the *original founder* of the Rosicrucian Order in Germany (speaking of C. R-C. as though he were an earthly person who invented and established the first lodge of Rosicrucians anywhere in the world) will know at once that the writer of the account is unfamiliar with the facts and has mistaken the allegorical story for an actual event. The other explanation of the Rosicrucian work, by an author of this calibre, may be easily placed in the same category of unreliability. And, when the seeker comes in contact with a mystical organization, or a "Rosicrucian" group, that claims that it has its *authority* and *power* derived from the organization started by

"Christian Rosenkreuz" in Germany, or that it is a *descendant from the original lodge* established by C. R-C. in Germany, he will know also that the claim must be fictitious and wilfully misleading; for the facts contained in this history will show that the Order was in existence in many lands before the popular new birth of the Order in Germany in the seventeenth century, and that any Rosicrucian student—and most certainly any leader of Rosicrucian activities connected with the genuine organization—would have the correct story and the correct facts which are available to all of those who are truly affiliated with the real organization.

CHAPTER V

THE POPULAR REVIVAL IN GERMANY

S INTIMATED in previous paragraphs of this history, the most popular and puzzling incident in the whole history of the Rosicrucian Order is in connection with the third or fourth revival of the organization in Germany. Coming as it did, at a critical time in the awakening of the religious consciousness of the people, and when various reforms were being instituted and attacks were being made upon older institutions, with a promulgation of ideas for newer ones, the announcement of the birth of the Rosicrucian Order for the new cycle in Germany was considered by many as a part of the general reform taking place throughout that country and other lands. The revival would never have become so popular nor attracted so much attention if it had not been that for the first time in the history of the Rosicrucian Order, the art of printing was freely used.

Such a use of printing was almost unique, and it naturally attracted the attention of persons who were easily convinced that great wealth and great power were back of this national and international program, and for this reason other pamphlets and booklets were written criticizing, commenting upon, and attacking the organization, as well as praising it and endorsing it.

The mass of literature resulting from the opening announcements of the German revival constitutes one of the very dependable sources of historical information regarding the Rosicrucians, and at the same time constitutes one of the deplorable problems that confronts every seeker for real information.

Many of the pamphlets and booklets issued by critics or by enemies of the organization—or even in some cases by persons who merely wished to attain prominence or attract attention through writing about the organization, without any real knowledge of the subject—resulted in a mass of misinformation, a great deal of which eventually found its way into encyclopedias and general histories. To this very day, the average newspaper, or magazine writer, or seeker for information regarding the organization, who turns to one of the standard encyclopedias or histories of literature, religion, science, or art, is very liable to come in contact with misleading statements based upon the critical essays written about the organization during this period of the German revival.

It is not my intention to take space in this present history to review the facts relating to the revival in Germany, but merely to call attention to the outstanding points connected therewith, because the real history of the revival, as well as the theoretical and misleading history, has been published in many books and can be found in many articles and essays dealing with Rosicrucianism.

The opening salute of that revival was the sudden and mysterious publication of a book briefly called *The Fama.* In just what year the original pamphlet entitled *The Fama Fraternitatis* was issued in Germany is really unknown; for there were so many editions in so many languages appearing in a number of different cities at slightly varying dates. Judging from copies which have been collected, one may see that the pamphlet appeared during the years 1610 to 1616, or even later. It is generally conceded that most of these were printed at Cassel, in Germany, although the English edition and the French edition were probably printed in other countries. As is natural with all of the ancient Rosicrucian literature, the authorship was veiled with a symbolic name, and a great deal of the literature of the period of revival in Germany was signed with the name of *Christian Rosenkreuz* if the pamphlet was in German, or with a similar name translated into other languages if published in foreign lands; or else the principal character telling the story in the announcements or proclamations bore this symbolical name. Of course, the name translated into our English means "a Christian of the Rosy Cross."

The pamphlets were addressed to the learned persons of the world, particularly of Europe, and appealed to the educated and cultured. It is very doubtful if any of the learned persons in Germany or other lands who read those pamphlets believed that the name *Christian Rosenkreuz* was the actual bona fide name of any person. However, today throughout the world we find thousands of persons, and especially those who have attempted to write misleading articles about the Rosicrucians, or who have attempted to found and organize commercial propositions selling so-called Rosicrucian books, who really seem to believe that the name *Christian Rosenkreuz* was the name of an individual, and that this individual was the real author of the *Fama* and other pieces of Rosicrucian literature, and likewise the *founder of the entire Rosicrucian Order* which had its beginning, according to their belief,

in this very establishment during the years 1610 to
1616.

The other general opinion regarding the authorship of these pamphlets is one which was born in
the minds of a great many persons who criticized
the organization during the seventeenth century.
They believed that an individual by the name of
Johann Valentin Andrea was the real author of the
Fama, and the later book called the *Confessio Fraternitatis R. C.*

In the year 1614, the *Fama* had attained na-
tion-wide popularity in its way, and had created
a real public sensation, and at that time Andrea
was but a young man of twenty-eight years. He
was born at Würtemberg, on August 17, 1586. He
was of a family devoted to the Lutheran form
of reformation, and although Andrea was raised
according to strict orthodox religious principles, he
did come under the influence and instruction of
a group of theologians and philosophers, two of
whom were mystically inclined, and one of whom
was one of the high officers of the Rosicrucian
Order in Germany. The public knew nothing of
his studies under this Rosicrucian teacher, but it
knew or heard something of his mystical viewpoints, and this was sufficient to make some start the

story that Andrea was the real author of the Rosicrucian pamphlets.

As has been explained heretofore, the Rosicrucian Order has always been subject to the law established by itself; one hundred and eight years of activity and one hundred and eight years of inactivity. We now have sufficient record, in the form of manuscripts, documents, and official papers not available or known to the German public in the seventeenth century, to show conclusively that the Rosicrucian Order was not born for the first time in the history of the world in Germany, in 1610 or 1614, but had existed in many lands for many centuries previous thereto, and had had cycles of activity and inactivity in Germany for several centuries before the revival to which we are referring. Even the *Fama* itself referred to the fact that the symbolical author of the manuscript, or the symbolical characters in the story, had been members of the organization centuries previous. All of this has been overlooked by those who still claim, especially in America, that a German whose true family name was *Christian Rosenkreuz,* invented and established the Rosicrucian Order, for the first time in the history of the world, in the years 1610 to 1614, in Germany.

One of the many well-established facts regarding the history of the Order, which proves the existence of the Order of the Rose Cross or Rosy Cross throughout Europe before 1610, is the story of the founding of one of the branches of the Rosicrucian activities.

Throughout Rosicrucian literature, reference will be found to peculiar initials and strange names usually connected with the title *Militia Crucifera Evangelica.* The "M. C. E." has always been a puzzle to those who have not worked through the complete history of the Order, and at the same time it has continued to be one of the most essential forms of Rosicrucian activities in many lands.

It may be that the following facts regarding the "M. C. E." will interest those of my readers who have never had the privilege of learning the real facts before, and it will probably set at rest the hundreds of questions that have been in the minds of Rosicrucian research workers for many years.

As stated above, the revival of the Rosicrucian work in Germany in 1610 to 1614, which constituted the beginning of one of the new cycles of one hundred and eight years, occurred when most of Europe was being torn by various forms of religious reformation and strife between church and state. Throughout each of the countries of Europe, various secret societies or military organizations had been formed to protest against the established activities of the larger church, or to stamp out the growing freedom of religious thought and practices of the so-called heretics. Thus we find that for many years before the revival of the Rosicrucian Order there had been established, in 1511 for instance, as typical of the many secret religious bodies, a *Holy League* composed of those persons who had pledged themselves to support the church against its critics, even to the extent of taking up arms and carrying on warfare in "the name of the cross." The *Holy League* was perhaps the most famous or powerful of these organizations, but there were so many others, and with so many different purposes or ends in view, that historians have been incapable of classifying them or even determining the real part that any of them played in the changes that were made. During all these years of strife and contention, the *cross* either as a Christian symbol or as adopted by the early Crusaders in the eleventh, twelfth, and thirteenth centuries was used as the standard under which the wars and other forms of persecutions were conducted. To the worshipper of the ancient cross, who had its *real symbolism* in his mind and heart, the use of the cross in the manner in which it was being employed by these contending organizations brought grief and deep sorrow.

Our records show that the Rosicrucians early protested against the cross being carried on staffs or painted on flags that were carried into the battles and into the fields of bloodshed, as well as into the plans and schemes for tortures and persecution. To the Rosicrucians, the use of the cross for such destructive work was not only irreligious and a sacrilege, but a mystical insult and a spiritual crime. It is easy to believe that the Rosicrucians, wherever they could avoid doing so, took no part in any of these religious strifes and contentions, and it is easy to believe that they never permitted themselves to carry any standard that bore the cross in public affairs.

Matters became so bad in connection with the use of the cross in this sorrowful way that finally the Rosicrucians decided to revive an ancient organization to defend the cross against its misuse. The idea of re-establishing this organization was born in the mind of the Grand Master of one of the inactive branches in Germany. His name was Simon Studion, and he was born at Urach in the state of Würtemberg in 1543, and later attained the high degree of Imperator in Germany. During the year 1586 he planned an international convention for the purpose of organizing a special body of Rosicrucians to defend the cross against its misuse in destructive and sorrowful activities. After communicating with the leading Rosicrucian officers in various lands, and receiving their wholehearted approval, a convention was called in Hanover, where was located the "silent" Grand Lodge of the Rosicrucians for that part of the country. The meeting was officially called "Cruce Signatorum Conventus," and its opening session was held on July 27th, 1586. Studion himself made the opening speech, reading the history of the original *Militia* formed in Palestine soon after the founding of the first Christian churches; and then introduced the high representatives from many lands and the legates from the many thrones which gave support to the movement. The records show that the convention and its plan was sponsored particularly and specifically by Henry IV, king of France and Navarre, who had received the "arms" of the ancient Militia through direct authority from the Militia in Palestine, Queen Elizabeth I of England, and the king of Denmark, as well as the nobility of other lands. The organization thus formed used the ancient name, *Militia Crucifera Evangelica,* and was established as an organization of loyal Rosicrucians who would defend the cross, not especially the Rosy Cross, but the ancient and much loved cross of all times, against its use in religious persecution, religious warfare, or destructive contests of any kind. Each who signed the great scroll at that convention became titled or knighted as a *Chevalier* and a secret worker to *protect* the Rosicrucian organization in its constructive activities, revive the pure mystical teachings of the Pristine Christians and Rosicrucians, and prevent persecution of any kind because of freedom of religious and scientific thinking. A few years later, when the records of activities of this great organization had been gathered from all lands, Studion compiled a great book of nineteen hundred and ninety-five (1995) pages, dedicated to Frederick, the Duke of Würtemberg, who was a Grand Master of the Rosicrucians. This book was called *Naometria,* and it was completed in 1604. This book is still in existence, and has been examined by eminent historians and quoted from quite freely. A Rosicrucian manuscript, entitled the *Wirtembergis Repertorum der Litterator,* a history of Rosicrucianism and alchemy, published in 1782-3, says, in part, of the *Naometria:* "Its reflections on the renewal of the earth and a general reformation to come breathe the Rosicrucian spirit—and it embodies real Rosicrucian doctrines."

A great part of the book is devoted to a history of the cross and its real spiritual and mystical significance, to the rose and its symbolical meaning, and to the special significance of the rose and the cross when united. In fact, on page 271, of the *Naometria,* there is an illustration of the joining of the two—the Rose and the Cross—and accompanying it the Latin phrase "Hierichuntis Rosa ex quotour ins Partes." The book contains also a complete outline of the Rosicrucian doctrines, reviving the ancient teachings of the Essenes, the first Christians, and the Rosicrucians, giving emphasis to the spiritual and mystical significance of the Rosicrucian ideals. It has never been copied or republished in any form, and constitutes one of the secret publications that has been examined only by eminent historians who have sought positive proof of the existence of such a book or such a Rosicrucian movement before the year 1610.

The *Militia Crucifera Evangelica,* as a defensive body within the Rosicrucian Order, still exists, and is the real secret organization within the Rosicrucian Order. Membership in it is limited to those who are well trained in the fundamentals of

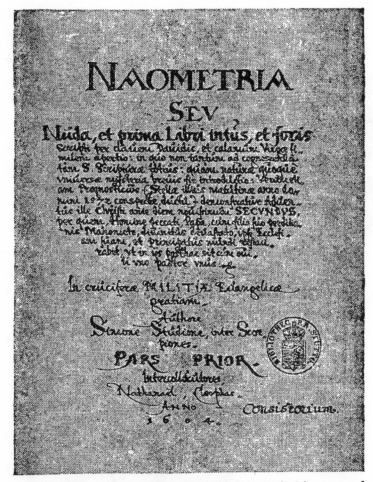

The above is a photograph of the original title page of the *Naometria* manuscript by Simon Studion. The original manuscript is in one of the large state libraries of Europe, where it is treasured as a rare possession. Note the reference to the Militia Crucifera Evangelica and the date 1604. This is the first text of Rosicrucian history in which this title page has ever been reproduced.

the Rosicrucian teachings, and to those who have pledged their entire lives in devotion to the Rosicrucian ideals, and especially to the support of the individual Imperator in each country where the Militia exists. It is the existence of such an organization that makes possible the continuous protection of the Rosicrucian Order, and it enables the Order itself to carry on its national and international secret activities in a conservative, uniform manner, to the glory of the Order and the preservation of the true, secret doctrines of Jesus. To be admitted and titled as *Chevalier* of this Militia is to receive one of the highest honors and highest acknowledgements in the Rosicrucian Order. The ranks of the Militia are open to both men and women who have been individually tested and tried for a number of years by the Imperator of the jurisdiction where each member lives.

An interesting point in connection with this is the fact that this organization and this convention of Rosicrucians was brought about by the cooperation of thousands of well-trained, tried, and tested Rosicrucians, and the first convention and meeting of establishment was held on July 27th, 1586, which was several weeks before Johann Valentin Andrea was born. The statement, therefore, on the part of those unacquainted with Rosicrucian history that Andrea was the author of the books that "established the first and only Rosicrucian Order in the world in Cassel, Germany, in 1610," appears ridiculous.

The real author of the pamphlets that brought about the revival in Germany was none other than Sir Francis Bacon, who was Imperator for the Order in England and various parts of Europe at the time. His other Rosicrucian writings, and especially his book the *New Atlantis,* admittedly his own work, clearly indicate the connection between Bacon and the publications issued in Germany between 1610 and 1616.

Conventicles, or special conclaves, of the Militia Crucifera Evangelica are held biennially at Rosicrucian Park at San Jose, California, U.S.A., the official See of the Supreme Grand Lodge of the Ancient and Mystical Order Rosae Crucis, the modern continuation of the ancient Rosicrucians. These conclaves are attended by chevaliers of the M.C.E. from throughout the world.

CHAPTER VI

THE BIRTH OF SEMI-ROSICRUCIAN ORGANIZATIONS

HE SPREAD of Rosicrucian activity throughout many lands and the attraction to its ranks of many notable characters brought the organization before the attention of men of other associations and affiliations. It was but natural that other secret societies or fraternal Orders would investigate the increasing activities of the Rosicrucian Order, and attempt to discover whether there was any invasion of their sacred rites by the Rosicrucians, or anything of value in the Rosicrucian work that might be added to their own rituals and forms of operation.

We will not consider at all the attempts made by various persons at various times to institute "Rosicrucian" lodges or bodies solely for the purpose of attracting the gullible or misleading the unwary. A number of such organizations came into existence in France, Germany, and England, but in each case their existence was very short and they left no records of importance.

We do find, however, that preceding the year 1870 the development of Freemasonic activity in England, with an increasing desire on the Continent to add more and higher degrees to the existing Masonic degrees, tempted many men of that organization to establish separate secret bodies or societies composed entirely of Masons, and in some cases new Orders or organizations were established with many degrees based upon Masonic symbols and requiring Masonic affiliations as a pre-requisite for affiliation in the new organization. The histories of Freemasonry deal extensively with this unfortunate situation throughout Europe, for these many bodies attaching themselves to Freemasonry or attempting to associate themselves with the Freemasonic ideals caused endless trouble and confusion. A few of the bodies thus formed became recognized eventually and carried on a very excellent work. It must be stated, however, that the average Freemasonic enthusiast of that period was a true seeker for *light* and arcane wisdom, and while he found much in the Freemasonic teachings to gratify his desires or satiate his hunger, many seemed to feel that there was more *light* and wisdom to be found elsewhere and especially in the secret, *mystic* schools which had their origin in the Oriental philosophies. Probably in those days, as today, many of those in the Freemasonic fraternity did not realize the vast amount of wisdom that is contained in their symbology and in their carefully veiled teachings. However that may be, the fact remains that many of the most prominent Freemasons congregated at different times in different places, and formed research bodies or groups devoted to the sole purpose of unearthing such additional teachings or arcane knowledge as might be found in the various *mystic* schools of the day.

It is not surprising, therefore, that a number of these men were attracted to the Rosicrucian Order, especially the English lodge, and were admitted therein and became enthusiastic students and workers. The time came, however, when some of these believed that further research of an independent nature might be carried on outside of both the Rosicrucian and the Freemasonic circles, and that members of both organizations might come together in a more social and informal manner at stated periods for the purpose of discussing the work and teachings found in both bodies.

Out of this belief was born a new organization in England, the activities of which, and the imitation of which, have caused considerable confusion in the minds of those persons seeking to trace the origin and development of the Rosicrucian Order.

It appears from definite historical records that some men of learning, and with minds adapted to research, united to establish what they intended to be a *Masonic* Rosicrucian Society. During their first discussion of the plans of organization it was clearly stated that application for membership in this new body would be limited to Freemasons, in good standing, who had mastered the elementary work of Freemasonry and were desirous of such philosophical knowledge as was available just beyond the limited teachings of their organization. The transactions of this organization, with minutes of its meetings, are to be found in the British Museum in London, but the most definite statements regarding its purposes and activities are found in a small historical treatise prepared by the Supreme Magus of the body, Dr. W. Wynn Westcott. It appears that after much discussion they decided to call their new society the *Societas Rosicruciana in Anglia,* which name, translated, would mean the *Rosicrucian Society in England,* and the initials of this title were used as a brief form of name in their literature. Hence the initials S.R.I.A. became significant among Freemasons during that period, and have contributed to considerable confusion in Rosicrucian records ever since.

It seems that the prime mover of the formation of this new society was Robert Wentworth Little, who is referred to in the records as a clerk at Freemason's Hall, and subsequently secretary of the Royal Institution for Girls. Freemason's Hall at that time was the national headquarters for the Freemasonic Brotherhood, and it contained a large library and archives of ancient books and manuscripts, to all of which Mr. Little had access. Nowhere in the early literature of this organization or in its early histories as published by them is there any reference to any of the organizers of the S. R. I. A. being initiates or members of any other Rosicrucian body or organization anywhere in the world. *This is a very important fact,* and its significance is emphasized by the statements of this society regarding the methods or means of its foundation.

In its official history, this S. R. I. A. says that the society was "designed" by Robert Wentworth Little, who "rescued" some rituals from the storerooms of Freemason's Hall. In other places there are statements indicating that Mr. Little found and *borrowed,* or as Mr. Waite, the Masonic historian, states it *abstracted* certain papers containing Rosicrucian ritual information preserved in the Grand Lodge library of Freemason's Hall, and that these papers had been discovered before him by William Henry White, who was Grand Secretary of the Freemasons until 1857. According to Dr. West- cott, Mr. White had received some "Rosicrucian" initiations in an English "Rosicrucian Lodge," but had never made any use of the ritual manuscripts which he had discovered in the Masonic Grand Lodge library. Waite calls attention to the fact that other records intimated that after Mr. White's re- tirement from the office of Grand Secretary, wherein he had charge of such secret or private manu- scripts as were not a part of the Masonic work, Mr. Little *borrowed* the Rosicrucian papers and called to his assistance a year or so later one Ken- neth R. H. McKenzie, who claimed that while he was in Germany he had been admitted by some "German adepts" into *some* of the "Rosi- crucian system," and had been licensed to form a group of Masonic students in England "under a Ro- sicrucian name."

To the sincere and careful student of Rosicru- cian history, the claims made by Mr. McKenzie seem peculiar, to say the least. Why some *German adepts* should admit an English person into just a *part* of the Rosicrucian work and then *license him* to establish a group of *Masonic* students in England under a *Rosicrucian* name, while there was a superior Rosicrucian body already active in England, is certainly incomprehensible. It would appear to be the first and only instance in Rosicrucian history where the Rosicrucian Order "licensed" anyone to establish a Masonic Rosicrucian body. And it is as inconsistent with Rosicrucian principles as would be the *licensing* of a Freemason to go into a foreign land and establish a Masonic body composed of Rosicrucians.

Dr. Westcott states also that the peculiar Rosicrucian papers that were taken from the Masonic archives were used to reconstruct a branch of the *Red Cross of Rome and Constantine,* as well as the foundation of the S. R. I. A.

The important points in this brief sketch of the foundation of the S. R. I. A. are: First, the fact that the Society was started by an individual without any charter or authority from the local Rosicrucian lodge in London, or any other superior Rosicrucian body in Europe; and second, that with some manuscripts of an indefinite nature a society was formed which did not adopt the universal name of the Rosicrucian Order or the universal symbol as used by the rest of the Rosicrucian fraternity throughout the Continent. In no other Rosicrucian records do we find any reference to any German branch that *licensed* Mr. McKenzie, and, therefore, we may believe that Mr. McKenzie's contact with the Rosicrucians, if real at all, was a contact with some of the temporary, clandestine, or imitation societies that flourished for short intervals in foreign sections.

Mr. Waite, in his English history of the Rosicrucian Order, gives little credence to Mr. McKenzie's Rosicrucian connections, and emphasizes the fact "That in 1866 McKenzie was a Mason only under some foreign and apparently unacknowledged Obedience." Mr. Waite, who is not only a Rosicrucian historian but an eminent Masonic historian and writer as well, plainly indicates the cloud that seems to cover the origin and foundation of the S. R. I. A., and shows that while it became a very worthy, learned, and highly respected organization of gentlemen seeking for arcane wisdom, enjoying a banquet and social evening once a month, it was not in any sense a part of the Rosicrucian organization throughout the world.

However, the S. R. I. A. in England continued to grow and called its first branch the *Metropolitan College*. We find that its principal officers were well-known Freemasons, and included a number whose names we shall mention later. Mr. McKenzie visited Paris some years later and there met one who was deeply interested in the Rosicrucian work and teachings, as a member of the regular Rosicrucian organization, known as Eliphas Levi, but whose name was Alphonse Louis Constant. Levi was invited to become a part of the S.R.I.A. in England, and did so with the belief that the founders were really sincere in their desire to delve deeply into Rosicrucian lore, and become neophytes of the Rosicrucian organization. A few years after his acceptance into the S. R. I. A., Levi evidently felt that his connections therewith were not proper in the face of his affiliation with the regular Rosicrucian Order, or else he discovered reasons for withdrawing. It is indicated that he had many arguments with the founders of the new English society, and disagreed with their viewpoints in many ways, and finally withdrew his membership. The records of the S. R. I. A. state that Levi incurred their displeasure by the publication of his several books on magic and ritual, but since these books have proved to be excellent and highly endorsed by mystics of many periods, such explanation does not seem to be justifiable. Levi passed through transition in 1875, and in the last years of his life was not connected with the S. R. I. A. in any way.

Other branches of the S. R. I. A. were established at Bristol, Manchester, Liverpool, and Yorkshire, and finally a branch was established in Canada. All of these branches were strictly limited to Freemasons. In fact, the ritual adopted by the S. R. I. A. for its initiations and ceremonies was quite distinct from the Rosicrucian ritual of the regular Order, and the fantastic names for the various grades were designed to appeal to Freemasons. The highest of these grades were limited to Freemasons who were in the higher grades of their own organization.

Prior to the establishment of a branch of the S. R. I. A. in Canada, which was intended to be under the British or English jurisdiction of the organization, a branch was authorized in 1880 to be known as the *Societas Rosicruciana in U. S. A.* According to some records, a few Freemasons living in Pennsylvania were granted permission to establish this American branch, but there is no record of its having existed very long in Pennsylvania, and in the meantime the Canadian branch carried on very successfully among the Freemasons in that part of North America.

We have seen the official copies of the charters issued by the Canadian branch which was known as the *Societas Rosicruciana in Canadiensis*. These charters were preserved in the House of the Temple of the Southern jurisdiction of the Scottish Rite of Freemasonry in Washington, D. C. They were issued by the Canadian branch of the S. R. I. A. to Brother Albert Pike and several others of the American Freemasonic organization, particularly because Albert Pike, the honored and respected writer of American Freemasonry, was a very thorough Rosicrucian student. The charter grants to Brother Albert Pike and others the privilege of establishing a Southern College of the S. R. I. A. in the United States, and it is worded as though the Canadian branch was unaware that a similar warrant for an American branch had been issued previously to the Freemasons in Pennsylvania. However, a controversy arose over the establishment of a second North American branch, and thereby hangs a very interesting story.

It must be borne in mind that these S. R. I. A. branches were not operating as a part of the ancient Rosicrucian Order, and by their own admission did not have the Rosicrucian rituals and teachings nor any warrant, charter, patent, or authority from the Rosicrucian Order of Europe and other lands. American Rosicrucian students were well aware of the fact that the Rosicrucian Order of Europe had previously authorized the establishment of true Rosicrucianism in America in the year 1693, and there were many living descendants of those first official Rosicrucians who objected to the establishment of Rosicrucianism in America in connection with any other organization and without warrant or proper rituals. But nothing was done to prevent the S. R. I. A. of England from maintaining a branch of its English work in America, especially in connection with Freemasonry, since it was recognized that the Masonic Rosicrucian society thus being established in America would cooperate with the desires of many of the Masons in giving them that additional light or knowledge along certain arcane lines which they desired, and which was highly praiseworthy. This did not in any way infringe the rights of the Rosicrucian Order. In fact, there was no conflict or discussion in that one regard, because the S. R. I. A. did not claim to have the *genuine* Rosicrucian teachings or ritual, and was, therefore, entitled to establish a branch of its English body in America.

The controversy referred to started between the various officials and members of the S. R. I. A.

and gradually involved the interest of all Rosicrucians; because the argument in regard to two establishments of S. R. I. A. under two different warrants was bringing the subject of Rosicrucianism and the Rosicrucian activities into unfavorable light among those who did not understand the situation. It appears that the gentlemen who were granted the privilege by the Canadian branch to operate in the United States finally withheld any action on their part, while the Brother who held the charter direct from England for the State of Pennsylvania, proceeded to organize a branch, and some spasmodic meetings of this branch were held without attempting to practice the Rosicrucian rituals or introduce the true Rosicrucian teachings. This was the situation existing in the United States when a third effort was made to establish the S. R. I. A. in America, and the third effort proved more successful, as we shall see from the following facts:

A number of Freemasons in America were admitted into the S. R. I. A. of England in its branch known as the *York College*. They petitioned the English headquarters for permission to continue the work in America under the charter that had been granted for Pennsylvania. They established a branch at Philadelphia and another in New York

City in 1880. Eventually these two American branches established a High Council of the society for the United States. This Council then chartered branches in Boston and Baltimore, in the spring of 1880, and another one in Vermont. Practically every officer connected with these establishments was a Freemason, and we must quote here the words of Dr. Westcott, the Supreme Magus of the English headquarters of the organization, who said in an address: "I have been asked to speak on the Rosicrucians because I have the pleasure to hold a high office in the *Rosicrucian Society* of England, so might reasonably be supposed to have studied the history of the Order. But to avoid misconception, I wish to say that *the S. R. I. A. is a Masonic body*—it is composed of Freemasons who have associated themselves in order to study the old Rosicrucian books in the light of history, and to trace the connection between Rosicrucianism and the origins of Freemasonry, the connection which has been alleged to exist by many historians belonging to the outer world." This statement by Dr. Westcott is taken from biographical sketches in the official literature of the S. R. I. A.

In September of 1889, after nine years of operation as a literary society with banquets, the new branches of the S. R. I. A. in America decided to reform and reorganized their body with the distinctive title "Societatis Rosicrucianae in the United States of America" (S. R. I. U. S. and not S. R. I. A.). Under this new form of name and constitution, the various branches accomplished very little, and the New York and Baltimore sections seemed to pass out of existence. One of the prominent characters initiated into the S. R. I. U. S. in Boston was Sylvester Clark Gould, who became the publisher of a small Rosicrucian magazine, and who sincerely sought to learn and master the real Rosicrucian teachings. We read in the official literature of this organization the following significant statement: "Membership in these Colleges was limited to Freemasons of the 32nd degree; quarterly meetings were held, and their sessions were devoted principally to banquets, with an aftermath of a literary and philosophical nature, with little if any attempt to exemplify the Rosicrucian degrees with the philosophy they embodied."

In other words, the society had nothing more of a Rosicrucian nature connected with it than the word *Rosicrucian* which they arbitrarily adopted in their title. This was practically true of the national headquarters of the organization in London, and records of this society show that when Rosicrucians belonging to the Rosicrucian Order became affiliated with the S. R. I. A. or the S. R. I. U. S., they did not continue to remain active for a very long period.

According to the literature of the branch established in America, Mr. Gould, who was their most illustrious American member, became "thoroughly awakened to the omission of the real Rosicrucian work, and having received the eighth degree of the society constituting him a provincial magus of the fraternity, engaged in special research work to recover the original rituals of the fraternity." He succeeded in corresponding with some Rosicrucian officers in Europe, and then undertook to revive the American branch of the S. R. I. A., which had become inoperative for a time. It was his intention to make the S. R. I. U. S. a typical Rosicrucian organization if he could secure the permission and authority of the Rosicrucian Order in Europe. According to the records of the S. R. I. U. S., the transition of Mr. Gould occurred on July 19, 1909, preventing the fulfillment of his personal ambitions in regard to the society, and the work of reorganization devolved upon a few of the other members who were still interested.

It should be noted that in the very month in which Mr. Gould passed to the Great Beyond, another American proceeded to Europe to secure permission to pursue the Rosicrucian work of the international Rosicrucian Order, and made his plea to the regular Order of Europe instead of petitioning the Masonic Rosicrucian society in England. The success of this plea we refer to in a future section of this history.

Those who followed Mr. Gould, after his passing, in trying to re-establish the S. R. I. U. S. in America, finally organized a new body with a different name. According to their official papers, they adopted the name *Societas Rosicruciana in America,* which gave them the old familiar initials S. R. I. A. as their official title. They adopted a revised constitution under this new name in 1919, which became effective January 1st, 1920. Their constitution stated that they were incorporated under three different classifications: first, as a church; second, as an academic institution; and third, as a fraternity. In their general literature, they stated: *"The Societas Rosicruciana in America,* therefore, is a continuation in direct succession from the High Councils of Anglia." In other statements it is said that the society "works in complete harmony and close association with the Masonic fraternity, and constitutionally its major officers are Masons of all rites and degrees." Furthermore, "the society, deriving from the English fraternity, was incorporated in 1912, and is therefore the active American branch of the Rosicrucian fraternity." These statements have been refuted by published articles in various magazines, and of course it is well known to all Freemasons and others that no other organization of any kind can be a part of Freemasonry unless it is operating under the Freemasonic title and symbolism. And, in regard to the S. R. I. A. in the United States being derived from the English fraternity of the same name or charter, or authorized by the same society in England, an article was published in the *Occult Review* of England in recent years, wherein the *Societas Rosicruciana in Anglia* denied that the society in America was sponsored by it or officially recognized by it. This denial was later acknowledged as correct by the American S. R. I. A., which leaves the American organization standing as a distinctly separate institution operating without any charter from the general Rosicrucian Order of Europe, or any Masonic Rosicrucian body of England.

This organization has, therefore, continued as an independent body, establishing a few branches in different cities, and continuing to make its appeal to Freemasons who enjoy purely philosophical discussions without any of the rituals or teachings as used in the various branches of the Rosicrucian Order of Europe and other lands.

Among several other American institutions using the name *Rosicrucian* in about the same manner that the S. R. I. A. of England and America have adopted it, is one which has also caused considerable confusion in the minds of those who attempt to trace the history and activities of the Rosicrucian Order. Since the name and term *Rosicrucian* is not protected by any patents or copyrights of any kind, it may be used in connection with other words for various purposes. Hence there may be Rosicrucian societies, Rosicrucian clubs, or Rosicrucian churches without having any authority from the Rosicrucian Order. It is interesting to note, however, that only one organization throughout the world uses the ancient title of *Rosicrucian Order* and this organization maintains its active branches in all lands, under the abbreviation of AMORC.

It appears from some historical records that a man by the name of Dr. P. B. Randolph, who was a student of the occult and mystical, came in contact with some Rosicrucian literature or essays prior to the year 1856 while in America. It appears that Dr. Randolph visited London in 1858 and

there met a student of mysticism known as Mr.
W. G. Palgrave, who claimed to be a member of
some esoteric Order in Europe, which was operating under a charter issued by a "Council of Seven."
Through this man he was introduced to Mr. Hargrave Jennings, Eliphas Levi, and several others
who eventually formed the High Council of the
original S. R. I. A. in England. Dr. Randolph was
initiated into this Masonic Rosicrucian body and
as an honorary member continued his tour, and returned to America. While in America he wrote
a number of books dealing with the subjects of
health, marriage, love, and sex hygiene, and in one
of them introduced a story about the mystic Rosicrucians, intimating that he was planning to establish some of the Rosicrucian Masonic work in
America on the basis of that which was being carried on by the S. R. I. A.

Because of the nature of his books, dealing in un-
usually plain language with subjects not generally
discussed in American literature, and certainly having none of the goodness and high idealism of the
S. R. I. A. (London) teachings, he was tried in
courts for such publications, and eventually abandoned his entire work because of the condemnation
of his writings. Mr. Arthur Waite, the eminent
Masonic historian of England, has this to say re-

garding Randolph's form of "Rosicrucian" activities
as considered by him:

"In respect of deception there is no question that
he was his own and his first victim if he thought that
his views and lucubrations might stand for authentic
Rosicrucian teachings. But in a judgment which
makes for justice it must be added that he revoked
his own claim on a vast antiquity. . . . It does not
appear that in the matter of the Rosy Cross he did
more than give a fresh circulation to some of the old
reveries, to the extent that he was acquainted with
these by common report and otherwise. . . . In
other and more hectic stories, he paraded flaming
accounts of the Brotherhood, its immemorial antiquity, its diffusion throughout the world, with
suggestions that its ramifications extended to un-
seen spheres . . . . I have worked through such of
his volumes as are available here in England, . . .
and have concluded that, mountebank as he was, he
believed in all his rant and was not lying con-
sciously when this stuff of sorry dreams was put
forward unfailingly as the wisdom of the Rosy
Cross. This is how it loomed in his mind, and this
is what it was in a dream, for it was a thing of his
own making. On this subject, he is his own refu-
table witness, affirming that 'very nearly all which

I have given as Rosicrucian originated in my own soul'."

Randolph eventually signed himself in some letters and papers as the "Supreme Grand Master of Eulis for the world," and a few of his friends tried to explain after his unfortunate transition through suicide that he believed himself to be a Grand Master of the "Triple Order." This term is not an official part of Rosicrucian terminology, and there are no documents or papers to be found in Europe indicating that he was ever authorized to establish anything of a Rosicrucian nature in America or elsewhere, and none of the historical records of the Order mentions his name or his branches as a part of the Rosicrucian history.

Randolph was succeeded by a Mr. Dowd, who tried to continue operating some of the branches which Randolph had established on the Pacific Coast and in several eastern cities, but, *according to their own records,* these branches constantly disbanded when the members thereof discovered that there were no real Rosicrucian teachings or rituals in the work, and insisted on withdrawing from the Randolph work and uniting with the regular foreign branches of the Rosicrucian Order. Mr. Randolph and his successors claimed that such actions constituted "treason," and for many years there were bitter quarrels and arguments within his branches over this point, with the branches disbanding and remaining inactive for years at a time. Mr. Dowd was succeeded by a Dr. Edward H. Brown, who likewise was unable to secure any of the Rosicrucian teachings, or maintain Randolph's scheme against the common criticisms and the bad reputation which his writings had brought upon their activities.

In a statement signed by Mrs. Randolph, and which appeared in a fraternal publication as a biographical sketch of the life of Dr. Randolph in 1917, it is said that Dr. Randolph was born in New York City on October 8th, 1825, and that his transition occurred in Toledo, Ohio, on July 29th, 1875; and she further stated that although he organized some branches as late as 1874, they "have long since become extinct."

According to Sedir, the well-known Rosicrucian historian, the work of Randolph was simply a society of "editions"—referring to the significant point that his work was mostly that of publishing various *editions of books* claiming to be Rosicrucian. This point is one which should be impressed upon the minds of every student of Rosicrucian history. The Rosicrucian Order has never been exclusively, or even primarily, a book publishing business, and a careful examination of the historical writings connected with the Rosicrucian Order shows that none of the books now famous as Rosicrucian manuscripts or official publications ever contained a complete outline of the secret teachings or rites of the Rosicrucians, and what is more important, never *claimed* to contain such things.

It has been a serious and universal law with the Rosicrucian Order that its secret teachings should never be published in book form, or offered for sale to the public, and there is no violation of this law that has ever been brought to our attention. On the other hand, there have been many who were not a part of the Rosicrucian Order, or even initiated in its teachings, who have attempted to commercialize the desires of seekers by the printing and selling of books which *claimed* to be "Rosicrucian textbooks" or books of Rosicrucian doctrines or teachings. It is a notable fact that *none of these books* has made any valuable contribution to mystical literature, and all have passed into oblivion and can hardly be found in the best libraries of Europe or America. This is true of Randolph's books, which claimed to be wonderful revelations of Rosicrucian teachings, but which today have no place in the real occultist's library and have not been considered worthy of preservation even in the great reference libraries of the world. Such books as these, catering to the gullibility of the seeker, and often misleading the worthy inquirer, are being published and sold in America today very freely, while Europe most naturally fails to support such publications. We have, for instance, in America, a book called *The Rosicrucians and Their Teachings.* This book was written by a New Thought leader, who has written many other books on various subjects and who is *not* a member of the Rosicrucian Order. The book contains none of the Rosicrucian teachings. Such books are harmless in themselves, and perhaps interesting to casual students of mysticism; but they have no place in any list of authoritative publications. It is for this reason that Sedir made his satirical remarks regarding Randolph's society of "editions." The good that Dr. Randolph did as a New Thought pioneer will live for many ages, but the failure of his Rosicrucian movement was due to a complete lack of authority, and no understanding of the Rosicrucian teachings.

Dr. Randolph's work was later taken up again by a Dr. R. S. Clymer, who claimed to be the "successor" to Randolph and to have inherited and acquired the Rosicrucian "authority" which Randolph had. Clymer followed the same plans adopted by

Randolph and conducted an organization consisting wholly of books, a number of which deal with love, marriage, and "sex regeneration," the latter being in such language as to be condemned in any Rosicrucian assembly, if not in any general assembly of ladies and gentlemen. He proceeded to carry on his work first under the name of a publication company, then under various names, avoiding the use of the complete name, or correct name, of the Rosicrucian Order, and devising entirely new and unique symbols for his Rosicrucian literature without infringing upon the correct symbols in any way. Dr. Clymer * continued to operate his sale of books and presentation of personal, "Rosicrucian" teachings under different names from his home in Pennsylvania, without having established any typical Rosicrucian temples anywhere in America, and without having any connection with the regular Rosicrucian Order and lodges of Europe.

It would be expected that Dr. Clymer's representations and maladroitly presented "teachings" and attacks on other movements would eventually attract the attention of the Supreme Council of the Rosicrucian Order of the World and the dignitaries of the Rose Croix of Europe. One of the first to voice a protest was the eminent F. Wittemans, avocat—

---

* For further details see page 156.

at the time, a member of the Belgian Senate—and renowned European historian of the Rosicrucian Order, his works on the Order being published in several languages. In a letter addressed to the Imperator of A. M. O. R. C. of North America, dated December 16, 1928, and referring to Dr. Clymer's writings, he said:

"I criticize very much such writings, which should not be issued by an occultist and prove by their self their hollowness. I will thus not mention them in my work—"

The combination of Dr. Clymer's synthetic Rosicrucian teachings and his insidious campaign of vilification and libel of the A. M. O. R. C., in the American jurisdiction aroused a spirit of defense and indignation on the part of the affiliated Rosicrucian bodies abroad. Coeval with Dr. Clymer's campaign of machinations against A. M. O. R. C., various individuals were establishing mystical and occult societies in America and elsewhere, having no true arcane or authoritative background, and misappropriating the time-honored signs, words, and terms of the esoteric, traditional, hermetic orders of Europe. This wholesale plagiarism was especially disastrous where the welfare of the humble seeker and the neophyte was concerned, for the protagonists of these movements were inept at presenting the mystical knowledge in a proper way, not having been initiated or prepared. Their "teachings" were a distorted and disorganized accumulation of certain of the noble precepts, damaging to the interests, and often the mentality of those who studied them. As nearly all of the true *Initiatory Orders* of the world functioned in harmony with each other, and as their concepts were based upon eternal truths, to a great extent paralleling each other, they were brought closer and closer together by the pressure of this rape of their Sacred Truths. What had been under way for some time finally came to pass, namely, a Federation of these societies and orders, for their mutual defense and the protection of their heritage. The Federation was duly instituted at Brussels, Belgium, on the 14th of August, 1934. It became officially known as the Federation Universelles des Ordres et Societes Initiatiques, known generally by the abbreviation, F. U. D. O. S. I. It consisted of the fourteen oldest arcane and mystical orders, each having as part of its rites certain initiations, which, because of their esoteric nature, produced mystical effects in the consciousness of the initiate.

The A. M. O. R. C. of North America was the only Rosicrucian body, of the few on this Continent so styling themselves, which was invited to become a member of this august Federation. The invitation was extended on the basis of such documentary authority and evidence of authenticity of the A. M. O. R. C., revealing its connection with the ancient fraternity of Europe, as existed in the archives of the Order in Europe, as well as in America. At the close of the conclave, which was attended by the highest officers of the respective Orders and the Imperators of the Rose Croix of the different jurisdictions, there was presented to the Imperator of North and South America, a document, signed and sealed with the emblems of the Orders participating, which reads, in part:

"(4)—that the only North American section of the A∴A∴O∴R∴R∴A∴C∴, duly authorized and recognized by the International Rosicrucian Council, and affiliated with the Supreme Council of the G∴W∴B∴ is that known in the Western world as A∴M∴O∴R∴C∴, with its S∴S∴ in the Valley of San Jose, California, of U. S. A., duly perpetuating the North American foundation of the Brotherhood, established in the City of Philadelphia in the year 1694, and having exclusive jurisdiction in North America."

Arthur Edward Waite, celebrated Masonic and Rosicrucian historian, in his history of the Rosy

Cross, also said of Dr. Clymer and his organization:

"It would serve no useful purpose to enlarge upon later foundations, like that of Dr. R. Swinburne Clymer, who seems to have assumed the mantle laid down by Randolph, or Max Heindel's Rosicrucian Fellowship of California. They represent individual enterprises which have no roots in the past."

The *Journal of the American Medical Association,* in its issue of December 15, 1923, said of Dr. Clymer: "Our records fail to show that this man was ever regularly graduated by any reputable medical college. In a paid notice that appeared in Polk's Medical Directory for 1906, Clymer claims the degrees of 'Ph.G.' and 'M.D.' He is classified as a 'Physio-Medicist' and a graduate of the 'Independent Medical College,' Chicago, 1898. The Independent Medical College was a diploma mill which sold diplomas to anyone who sent the cash. It was finally declared a fraud by the federal authorities and put out of business."

In 1939, Dr. Clymer, after making what appears to have been his *first* trip to Europe, although claiming for years previously that his organization was affiliated with the authoritative Rosicrucian Order of the World, said in correspondence: "I have just returned from Europe, where a meeting of the International Confederation was held in Paris, and articles signed by the many European organizations." It will be noted that the *International Confederation,* to which Dr. Clymer referred, appears to have been modeled after the F.U.D.O.S.I., established in 1934, to which Dr. Clymer and his organization were *not invited* because of ineligibility. Five years later, therefore, or in 1939, Dr. Clymer either had another existing body of equal dignity, tradition, and authenticity recognize his small association, *or* he went to Paris *to invent* such a body and *to confer upon himself* the European recognition which he did not have and needed.

That the latter was the case is borne out from the following evidence: Hieronymus, the Imperator of the Rose Croix of Europe, and Jean Mallinger, an avocat of the Belgian Court of Appeals and Secretary of the F. U. D. O. S. I., through the Corresponding Secretary of the Order in France, wrote to the Imperator of the A. M. O. R. C. of North America that they officially had no knowledge of any such *International Confederation of Rosicrucians,* to which Dr. Clymer referred, of its meeting in Paris, or its purported signing of articles. In essence, however, they stated that if such a meeting were held, it was *clandestine,* and any articles which those attending adopted and signed would have no more legal weight with the Rosicrucian Order throughout the world than the mere blank paper upon which they were written.*

Dr. Clymer's claims that his organization was the only true representative body of Rosicrucian philosophy in the Western world have been challenged upon numerous occasions by the executive officers of A. M. O. R. C. He was asked to meet the Chief Executive, or Imperator, of A. M. O. R. C. in public debate, at a place and at a time of his own selection. Upon such occasion, he was to be permitted to introduce all materials, documents, and papers, decrees and charters, which he might have in his possession, to substantiate his claims; and A. M. O. R. C. would do likewise. As a gesture of good faith in making the challenge, A. M. O. R. C. offered to pay all the expenses incident to such debate.

Dr. Clymer's refusal, *in writing,* a number of times, is part of the evidence which A. M. O. R. C. possesses of his *disinclination* to bring about a fair and final solution of this problem and disputatious matter. In essence, he stated in his correspondence

---

*See statement about Clymer and his international Confederation appearing in the Manifesto issued by the F. U. D. O. S. I. in Brussels in 1939.

and in books which he wrote upon the subject, that no purpose would be served by such a *public* disclosure. On the other hand, he continued to make one-sided, distorted misrepresentations of the facts in books, which he himself circulated to public libraries, institutions, organizations, and societies. I leave it to the reader, therefore, to judge the *conduct, fortitude,* and *motives* of Dr. Clymer.

In considering other semi-Rosicrucian movements in America, we find little in any of the Rosicrucian histories of Europe to support their claims to Rosicrucian association. That which was most popular in past years was the Rosicrucian *Fellowship,* established by Mr. Max Heindel. Mr. Heindel was at one time a student of the occult. In his desire to learn more about the Rosicrucian teachings, he went to Europe to seek affiliation with the Order. He became discouraged by the many obstacles presented, and finally became a personal student of Mr. Rudolph Steiner, the eminent *Theosophist,* who was an unaffiliated student of Rosicrucian history and principles. Mr. Steiner was at that time inaugurating the work of a new organization of his own creation, and Mr. Heindel became one of his enthusiastic students. Mr. Heindel claimed that in addition to this short period of study in Europe, he had a *"psychic initiation"* into the

Rosicrucian Order during a *dream* or a *trance,* whereby he was *authorized* (!) to proceed with the work of bringing Rosicrucian philosophy to America and later given permission through the same unnamed and unknown Masters to write a personal outline of his opinions of the Steiner teachings and issue this to the American public in regular book form.

These claims to authority by Mr. Heindel, and his subsequent organization, have been refuted by the Grand Master of the Rosicrucian Order of Germany. In a document, dated in Berlin on June 3, 1930, and now in the archives of the A. M. O. R. C. of America, and which was signed not only by the German Rosicrucian Grand Master, but by high Civil authorities of the German Government, there appear the following statements in both the English and German languages: "The irrevocable proof that the claims of the above-mentioned leaders of the Rosicrucian Fellowship, of Oceanside, are false can be ascertained by a perusal of the Rosicrucian Fellowship publications, which have also appeared in German translation. . . . Max Heindel has no connection with this only authentic German Rosicrucian Fraternity, whose origin goes back to their forefathers, the Deutsche Gottesfreunde, a brotherhood of high adepts, of the 13th and 14th centuries, from whom our tradition descends in direct and continued line through descent and the ties of the Order. . . . An initiation through psychic-spiritualistic manipulations of the kind Max Heindel claims to have received is not recognized by the true German Rosicrucian Fraternity."

He returned to America, and in 1911 established his printing plant and offices in a very small city of Southern California, and before his transition in 1919 had written a number of books dealing with an outline of his personal "Rosicrucian" beliefs, which are claimed to be a form of "Christian philosophy." So, once again, America was presented with a representation of so-called Rosicrucian doctrines through commercialized books, selling to anyone who had the price, dealing with many subjects not taught in the regular Rosicrucian lodges of Europe or elsewhere. Mr. Heindel made no attempt to establish lodges throughout the country, as is customary with the Rosicrucian Order in every land, for, of course, he had no authority from the Order in Europe to do so, and he in no way conducted the work as it is conducted by the Rosicrucian Order.

Unquestionably, the work of Mr. Heindel was inspirational and added to the interesting mystical literature of America, but the name of his personal organization, and the fact that all his work was conducted through the sale of books, plainly indicated to the Rosicrucian seeker that the work of Mr. Heindel, like that of several others, was unofficial from the Rosicrucian point of view, and "Rosicrucian" only in name. His widow attempted to continue the Fellowship after his transition, but internal difficulties arose and she withdrew from all connection with the Fellowship in the early part of 1932, while a few of its former students attempted to hold together the remnants of an organization that reduced itself to a mere personal interpretation of Christian teachings.*

Thus we have written of the various semi-Rosicrucian, or unofficial, organizations existing in America, including the "Masonic" Rosicrucian activity which started in England and made many attempts to establish itself in the United States. All of these bodies have done good work in their particular fields, and, aside from the objectionable sex teachings that are found in a few of the books issued by some of these organizations, their publications undoubtedly start many casual students of occult science on a path that leads eventually to the higher teachings.

---

* Apparently because dissension might have meant dissolution of the Fellowship, an accord was reached with the Board of Directors and Mrs. Heindel returned.

CHAPTER VII

THE FIRST ROSICRUCIANS IN AMERICA

E HAVE just been speaking of semi-Rosi-crucian bodies in America, but we must not overlook the first *genuine* Rosicrucian body to come to America. The brief facts given herewith are taken from two excellent books. First, that by Mr. J. F. Sachse, who was an heir and descendant of the first Rosicrucians to establish an official branch of the work in the United States, and second, from Mr. Arthur Waite's history of the Rose Cross Order. According to these two books, and the many other books quoted by them in their histories, a movement was started in Europe in 1693, as a result of previous plans to send a colony of leaders in the Rosicrucian work from the principal European branches to America, not only to found a Rosicrucian colony but to establish the Rosicrucian sciences, arts, and trades. The plan had its inception in the book called the *New Atlantis* written by Sir Francis Bacon while he was Imperator of the Rosicrucian Order in Europe, and which plan was later worked out in detail by the principal lodge of the Rosicrucian Order in London known as the *Philadelphia Lodge* or the *Philadelphic Lodge,* named after the city in the East where one of the original mystery schools was located.

In the fall of 1693, the tourists started out in a specially chartered vessel called the *Sarah Maria* under the leadership of Grand Master Kelpius, who was connected with the *Jacob Boehme Lodge* of the Rosicrucians in Europe, and with other officers from the Grand Lodge of the Rosicrucians in Heidelberg. They reached the city that is now known as Philadelphia, and to which they gave that name, in the first months of 1694, and built many buildings in what is now known as Fairmount Park, and later they moved further west in Pennsylvania.

Mr. Sachse, in his monumental work on these early Rosicrucians, says of this event: "Ten years later June 24th, 1694, Kelpius and his chapter of Pietists or true Rosicrucians landed in Philadelphia, walked to Germantown, and finally settled on the rugged banks of the Wissahickon."*

Many of their own books and manuscripts prepared in their own printing plant are still preserved in the historical collections of various historical societies of Pennsylvania, and by the descendants of

---

The German Pietists of Pennsylvania, by Sachse, page 4.

early governors of the state. Mr. Sachse and Mr. Waite have examined many of these manuscripts and books and find in them the undoubted connections with the Rosicrucian Order, and the presentation of the true Rosicrucian teachings. Mr. Waite discusses at length the Rosicrucian manuscripts used by these American pioneers and shows that they were the genuine secret teachings of the Order, and that the activities and regulations of the men and women forming the colony coincided with the standard activities of other Rosicrucian branches. It was here that many important American institutions were established, and that valuable contributions to the scientific and art foundations of the United States were laid. The list of eminent Americans who became affiliated with the Rosicrucian activities during the first century of its existence in Philadelphia reads like the roster of American patriots and leaders. Benjamin Franklin and Thomas Jefferson were but two of the outstanding figures in the activities of this national headquarters of the Rosicrucians in America.

"In that retired valley beside the flowing brook the secret rites and mysteries of the true Rosicrucian Philosophy flourished unmolested for years, until the state of affairs brought about by the American Revolution, together with pernicious Sunday legislation which also discriminated against the keepers of the scriptural Sabbath day, gradually caused the incoming generation to assimilate with the secular congregations."*

It would take too many pages in this history even to outline the many unique forms of activities which they created in a spirit of assisting to build up a new nation in a new land.

We must call attention again to the fact that this first colony came to America in accordance with the rules and regulations of the 108-year cycle of the Rosicrucian Order. Having started their movement toward America in 1693, it was only natural that 108 years later, or in 1801, this first American movement should close its outer public activities and start its cycle of 108 years of retirement and secret activity. So we find, according to the records, that in 1801 the large colony of Rosicrucians in Philadelphia dispersed and proceeded to various parts of the United States where small branches had been prepared even as far west as the Pacific Coast. The principal buildings in Philadelphia were abandoned, and the members continued to carry on their work in silence. Children were carefully trained in the teachings, and as they reached adult-

---

*The German Pietists of Pennsylvania, by Sachse, pages 7-8.

hood were initiated secretly into the organization so that their descendants might also carry on the work.

It was well known that as the 108-year cycle of silence and secrecy closed in the year 1909, the Order would again be authorized and chartered in a public manner and therefore, documents, papers, seals, and jewels were carefully handed down from one generation to another in anticipation of the coming of the year 1909. And, just as Mr. J. F. Sachse became the custodian of many of the manuscripts and jewels, so other descendants, notably those who assisted in the re-establishment of the new Order in 1909, possessed certain papers or "keys" which were useful in re-establishing or bringing to birth again the Rosicrucian Order in America, in its new cycle.

Thus we close this section of the history, but call attention to the fact that during the years 1800 to 1900 the Order in France, Germany, England, Switzerland, Holland, Russia, Spain, and in the Orient, was carrying on with increasing activity, but under very difficult conditions. It was found necessary, in most foreign lands, to continue the extreme silence and secrecy originally established because of the political persecution that was directed toward every sort of secret organization devoted to the promulgation of advanced knowledge and the higher laws. Despite such difficulties, the records show that in France, England, and Germany especially, the organization operated a great many branches with ever-increasing membership; and as the year 1909 approached, many men and some women journeyed to Europe to contact the Rosicrucian Order. Among these were a few eminent Freemasons, who sought to revive the "Masonic" Rosicrucian studies, and others who sought permission or authority to assist in the new birth of the 1909 cycle. The success of their missions, and the result of their activities, will be referred to in the next section of this history.

CHAPTER VIII

THE PRESENT ROSICRUCIAN ORDER IN AMERICA

IN WRITING this section of the history, I find that I cannot avoid using the first person pronoun because of my own intimate connection with the activities to be described, and I trust that the reader will understand this and overlook the personal element.

I have said that as the year 1909 approached, many men and women journeyed to France or other parts of Europe seeking not only initiation into the Order, but some official permission to aid in the establishment of the Order again in the United States, for its new cycle.

In France, during the years from 1880 onward, the Order became very active, because the year 1880 was apparently the beginning of a new cycle of the Rosicrucian activities for several of the countries, and records show that in the years 1900 to 1909 the Rosicrucian branches were many, and very active indeed, especially in France. It was only natural, therefore, that those students of Rosicrucian history, and those who had been partially initiated into the work as descendants of earlier members of the Order, should look to France and its high development in the Rosicrucian activities for aid in their plans and desires. As in other lands at other periods, a number of semi-Rosicrucian bodies had come into existence in France during the early part of the twentieth century, and many of these gradually affiliated with the Rosicrucian Order and adopted the strict rules and regulations of the ancient fraternity. A few of them, however, continued to use their previous titles even after affiliation with the Order, and this caused some confusion in the minds of those who journeyed to France seeking the genuine movement.

Many veiled stories regarding the Brotherhood had appeared in France, notably those by Eugene Sue, and Émile Zola. These informed the seekers of the existence of certain Rosicrucian activities which contained clues that enabled the determined seekers finally to contact the proper officials. From the seventeenth century onward, the Order in France had adopted the French term *Rose Croix,* in preference to the Latin term *Rosae Crucis.* We find even in Wassenaer's *Historisch Verhael* published in 1623, mention of the *Ordre de la Rose Croix* in France, with connections with members and other branches of the Order in Spain, Italy, England, Switzerland, Germany, Flanders, and other lands; and many prominent persons are mentioned in several French histories as having been active in the Order previous to the new cycle of 1880. I refer to such persons as Garasse, Gaultius, Naude, Richelieu, Louis XIII, king of France; and many others, even Descartes. Other records show that Jacques Rose organized before his transition in 1660 one of the newest and largest branches of the Rose Croix, and of course there were such famous leaders of the work in France as *le Comte de Gabalis,* Martínez Pasquales, and Louis Claude de Saint-Martin.

The very complete history of the Rosicrucian Order written in French and other languages by Brother Wittemans, a member of the Belgian Senate, and an honorary member of our Order here in America, contains very interesting facts regarding the activities of the Order in France during the twentieth century. Among the independent organizations in France after 1900 were a branch of the S. R. I. A. of England, the "Masonic" Rosicrucian society referred to previously, the Hermetic Order of the Golden Dawn founded in 1887, and *l'Ordre Cabbalistique de la Rose-Croix.* The latter organization contained a number of officers connected with the regular Rosicrucian Order, and this cabalistic body devoted itself to a limited list of subjects for scientific research and did not claim to be a part of the regular Rosicrucian Order. It was therefore never considered a clandestine body.

There was also an independent organization known as *la Rose Croix Catholique,* which attracted the interest of many Roman Catholics who were misled into the belief that it was a separate organization for them. On the other hand, there was also a Rosicrucian group quite independent under the leadership of Frater Castelot, who was, and remained until his transition, a member of the regular Order in France, and one of the honorary members of our Order here in America.

Frater Castelot was one of the most eminent and dearly beloved workers in the art of alchemy, devoting his time and interest to the study of alchemical problems with the few who were in his independent organization. He demonstrated in their group laboratory the possibility of transmutation in accordance with the Rosicrucian teachings and succeeded in producing gold, as told in a story published by our Order in our official magazine, the *Rosicrucian Digest.*

However, the real Order, as established throughout the world, had several official branches in

France as national headquarters. One of these was the "Secretariat" in Paris, while another was a College of Rites at Lyons, originally established by Cagliostro, and the national Council Chambers and temple, with the national archives in the environs of Toulouse, the ancient site of the first Rosicrucians established in Europe.

The meetings that were held in the various special branches of the Order in parts of France were as secret and veiled as were the activities at the larger national offices. It was difficult to locate a Rosicrucian lodge or identify a Rosicrucian member anywhere in Europe, a situation which has greatly changed in the last twenty-five years.

A survey of the history of the various occult movements that find moral and psychic support from the Great White Lodge shows that in the year 1909 more of the mystical movements of the world were reborn, revised, or changed in their form of activity than in any other year of occult history. It was in this year that Mr. Heindel of the semi-Rosicrucian independent society in America went to Europe to attempt to secure Rosicrucian information, and instead became a student of Mr. Rudolph Steiner, and his revised form of theosophy. It was also in the year 1909 that Mr. Gould planned to go to Europe to secure the true Rosicrucian rituals and teachings for his branch of the S. R. I. A. in the United States. And other leaders of other movements journeyed to Europe during this year, or received instructions from foreign branches in this year, to revise or renew their activities.

It was in 1909, also, that I made my visit to France for a similar purpose. For many years I had held together a large body of men and women devoted to esoteric and metaphysical research along Rosicrucian lines. As editor of several esoteric magazines, I had made contact with various Rosicrucian manuscripts and had discovered that I was related to one of the descendants of the first Rosicrucian body in America—that which had established itself in Philadelphia in 1694. This gave me access to many of their old papers, secret manuscripts, and teachings. These we discussed, analyzed, and attempted to put into practice. Among ourselves, the society, composed of several hundred persons in professional life, was known as *The Rosicrucian Research Society*. Among the many prominent persons then affiliated and holding active positions as officers were I. K. Funk, president of the Funk and Wagnalls Publishing Co. (publishers of the *Literary Digest*), "Fra" Elbert Hubbard, of the famous Roycrofters, who was deeply interested in the work to the very day of his transition, and Ella Wheeler Wilcox, the famous mystical writer, who later became a member of the Supreme Council of AMORC, which position she held until the time of her transition. Others of equal prominence, who were active members, are still members in high degrees of the present AMORC. The meetings of the Society were held monthly from 1904 to 1909 in New York City. Realizing that we were not yet chartered or authorized to use the name *Rosicrucian,* the society operated publicly under the name of *The New York Institute for Psychical Research.*

Just before 1909 there applied for membership in our society one who presented papers proving appointment as "Legate" of the Rosicrucian Order in India. Many weeks of close association with this member revealed the fact that I might be successful in my search for some form of authority to introduce the true Rosicrucian work in America at the right time. Every means of communication with any official of the Order in foreign lands was denied to me until early in the year 1909 when I was informed that the year for the public appearance of the Order in America was at hand and that definite arrangements for the new cycle had been completed. The Legate from India encouraged me to follow the urge that had actuated me for six or more years, regardless of any obstacles or trials that might tend to discourage my unselfish aims.

Therefore, I went to France in the summer of 1909 and after a brief interview with one who refused to commit himself very definitely, I was directed to various cities, and in each case redirected until I finally approached a definite contact in Toulouse. There I eventually found that my plans and desires had been anticipated and known for some time. I was permitted to meet not just one of the officers of the French Rosicrucian Order, but a number, as well as some who were members of the international Council of the Rosicrucian bodies of various European nations. At a regular Council meeting, and at several special sessions of the Order in other cities held in the months following, I was duly initiated and given preliminary papers of instruction to present to others whose names had been given to me. I was also instructed to arrange to hold preliminary foundation meetings for the purpose of organizing a secret group of workers, who would receive further instructions from Legates of the Order in India and Switzerland. These instructions were signed by Count Bellcastle-Ligne, the secretary of the international Council, and the venerable La-salle, the well-known author of many historical Rosicrucian documents, and Grand Master of the Order Rosae Crucis or *Rose Croix of France*. Before leaving France I had the pleasure of meeting several of the highest officers, and met in America, on my return, the Legate from India, who presented to me the jewels and papers which had been preserved from the early American foundation.

Throughout the years 1909 to 1915, many official Council sessions were held in my home and the homes of others, with men and women present who were descendants of early initiates of the Order, and a few of whom were initiates of the Order in France during the years 1900 to 1909. In 1915 the first official public *manifesto* was issued in this country announcing the birth of a new cycle of the Order, and immediately thereafter the first Supreme Council of the Order was selected from among hundreds of men and women who had been carefully selected during the preceding *seven years*. At the first official sessions of this American Supreme Council, officers were nominated and I was surprised to find that the Legate from India had been instructed to nominate me as the chief executive of the Order because of the work I had done during the seven years in organizing the new foundation. Well-qualified persons were elected to other executive positions in the Order, and copies of the French constitution of the Order and official documents were presented to committees for translation and adoption in a form to fit American conditions.

These meetings were followed by the first initiation of new members, the report of which to the French High Council brought a document of sponsorship for the American branch signed by the principal French officers. As with every new cycle in each land, the first years of its activity are under the sponsorship of some well-established jurisdiction, and so for a time this new cycle of the American Order operated under the sponsorship of the French jurisdiction.

It must be noted that from the very start, and with the issuance of the first public manifesto, the correct name of the international Rosicrucian organization was used, namely, the *Ancient Mystical Order Rosae Crucis*. This is a slightly abbreviated form of the original Latin name, *Antiquus Arcanus Ordo Rosae Rubeae et Aureae Crucis,* and the initials AMORC were immediately used as well as the true and original symbol of the Rosicrucian Order—the golden cross with but *one red rose* in its center.

At this time, and especially during the years 1915, 1916, and 1917, there were in existence in America several forms of semi-Rosicrucian movements, namely, the S. R. I. A., and the Rosicrucian *Fellowship* founded by Mr. Heindel. One will note that the S. R. I. A. was using the unique independent name of *Society* of Rosicrucians, rather than the ancient name of the Rosicrucians, which body always used the name *Rosicrucian Order* as used by us; and the S. R. I. A. symbol was very different from the symbol used by us. The Rosicrucian *Fellowship* likewise had adopted a name that was not that of the regular organization throughout the world, and for its symbol had created a new and independent device consisting of a cross with a *garland of seven roses* around it instead of only *one rose* in its *center*. Both of these organizations were publishing their teachings in book form, and were carrying on a work that was undoubtedly of value to students of general occultism. The very earmarks of their organizations—their distinctive names and symbols—differentiated them from the ancient organization, and the fact that they published and sold books claimed to contain the Rosicrucian teachings, put them in a different category from any of the other Rosicrucian Branches of Europe or else-where.

Therefore, the AMORC proceeded with the ancient customs and practices by publishing no books of teachings, but insisted that all who desired to study the work of the Order must join with and help form regular lodges or chapters in various localities.*

So successful was this form of activity during 1916 that branches were established from coast to coast, and from Canada to Mexico. By the summer of 1917 there were so many branches of AMORC in existence and carrying on the work with such enthusiasm that a National Convention was called for one week at Pittsburgh, Penna. Here hundreds of delegates from the branches, and members of the Order, assembled officially to acknowledge the existence of the Order and to finally adopt a National Constitution.

A committee was selected, composed of ten or more well-known Freemasons, who were eminent in the sciences and professions and who were *fa-*

---

*The books which the A. M. O. R. C. publishes, on various mystical, philosophical, and metaphysical topics, do not contain the official teachings of the Rosicrucian Order.

miliar with ritualistic and fraternal law, to examine the translated and revised French constitution of the Order, for adoption in America. This committee rendered its report, and the National Constitution of AMORC was adopted at the sessions of the convention, paragraph by paragraph. The Committee later signed a document stating that their experience with the work as members of the Order, and their familiarity with the claims and teachings of the Order, proved to them that the Rosicrucian work as issued by the AMORC was distinctly different from anything that they had contacted in their other affiliations, and worthy of the deepest and most profound study on the part of every seeker for the greater light. Other matters were officially established by this great convention, and thereafter the organization continued to grow throughout the United States, Canada, and Mexico.

This increasing activity resulted in a proclamation being issued at the International Convention of Rosicrucians held in Europe, establishing North America as a complete jurisdiction of the international organization, and it was then no longer necessary to operate as a branch of the French body.*

Eminent Rosicrucian officers of France, notably Monsieur Verdier, the commander-in-chief of the Illuminati of the Rosicrucians in France, visited the Order in America and left papers of approval and recognition. These were followed later on by a document issued by the International Convention held in Switzerland, appointing the national headquarters of the Order in North America as a branch of the international body. This latter document is one of the most important in the archives of the American headquarters.

During the years 1918 to 1925, the Imperator for the Order in America was honored with various degrees in the French organization, and in 1926 attended the next session of the International Conventions held both in Toulouse and Switzerland, receiving other appointments and honors; and finally in Paris during the same year, at a high reception given by a Congress of the most notable

*The international jurisdiction of A. M. O. R. C. has since been increased to include all of the countries of The Americas, British Commonwealth, France, Germany, Holland, Italy, Switzerland, Sweden, and Africa. The jurisdiction's addition was by authority and proclamation issued during the 1934 International Convention and Congress of the Rose-Croix of Europe and affiliated bodies held in Brussels, Belgium. See page 150 for further details of International Conclaves of Rosicrucians, in which the A. M. O. R. C. of America was the only Rosicrucian participant from the Western world.

of all the Rosicrucian officers of Europe, he was acknowledged as one of the highest officers of the Rosicrucian work. At the same time these high officers of the French Order, who are also high officers of other fraternal organizations in Europe, were made honorary members of the American Order, and official papers exchanged to verify these appointments.

The Order in America, known by the general international name of the Order as AMORC, continues to function strictly in accordance with the ancient traditions and in affiliation with all other recognized branches. The Imperator of the AMORC in North America is the only official American delegate to the International Rosicrucian Conventions. After the Great World War of 1914-17 the Order in various parts of Europe, Asia, and Africa had to operate under strict surveillance and with great secrecy, while here in America conditions were favorable to an open and frank operation of all Rosicrucian activities.* Hence the

---

*This refers to the first world war. During the second world war an edict existed prohibiting the continuation of any secret, philosophical, or mystical fraternal orders and societies in France and in all of the countries occupied by the Nazis. They particularly sought to suppress the Rosicrucians and Freemasons. Once again, therefore, there was the attempt to extinguish the light of truth. Communications from the French Grand Secretary of the Order were irregular, veiled, and most of the time transmitted by means of the underground.

principal propaganda of the Rosicrucians may be carried on in this country without interference; for this reason the work in North America has grown to such an extent that the American AMORC today is the largest metaphysical and mystical organization in the Western world.

Adhering to the ancient traditions, the AMORC sells no books claiming to contain the secret teachings and does not sell its services at any price. Membership is limited to those who are carefully examined and tested with preliminary studies for many months and then finally admitted into regular membership. The teachings are given freely to those who are members, and no fees are charged for degrees or titles as with organizations operating on a commercial basis. An official magazine called the *Rosicrucian Digest* is sent from the international jurisdiction of AMORC to all members, thereby keeping every one of its many thousands of students well acquainted with the general activities of the Order in America and affiliated lands. The Order now owns Egyptian temples and lodge rooms throughout the United States, Canada, the British Commonwealth, Mexico, Central and South America, Europe, and Africa. It possesses property devoted exclusively to the great work, and carries on a number of humanitarian activities under various names in order to avoid publicity in connection with such matters as are of no public concern.

The Supreme Temple was first located in New York City, but in 1918 was moved to the Pacific Coast because of property secured there which had been originally owned by the first organization established in America, and which was eventually transferred to the present Order. After establishing administration offices and a Supreme Temple in San Francisco, the executive offices were moved, in 1925, for a period of two years, to Florida, in order to help strengthen the work in the Southeastern part of the United States. An agreement was made with the large membership on the Pacific Coast that the Grand Lodge would return within two years to the West, and so in one day less than two years the organization, with the entire executive staff returned to the Pacific Coast to occupy its own property at its present site in San Jose, California, where the Order maintains a beautiful park and instruction facilities which include the following: a large Egyptian Museum and Art Gallery built upon authentic Egyptian designs and which contains the finest collection of Egyptian and Babylonian antiquities in Western United States, a beautiful Egyptian-styled Supreme Temple, a modern Planetarium that houses the latest in planetarium equipment, a Science Museum, a University complex with laboratories and classrooms, a sound Studio in which films and sound recordings are made, a Research Library, an Auditorium, and extensive administration buildings. Unlike other secret organizations of a mystical nature, the AMORC in North America during its entire history has had very little unfavorable publicity purporting to discredit its teachings and practices. It has never been involved in any political disputes.

THE PILGRIMAGE TO EGYPT

Early in 1928, the Imperator for North America received official notice of several important national and international meetings that were to be held by the various Rosicrucian bodies of Europe and Egypt during the spring of 1929.* Desiring to have the highest officers of the organization in North America meet many of the high officers of the Order in foreign lands, the Imperator planned a pilgrimage to Egypt and proceeded to select members from the various groups and lodges throughout North America who could accompany him on his trip. The members finally selected represented thirty-one different cities in North America, covering nineteen jurisdictions and every grade and degree of the work. Among these were

*The Imperator here designated was Dr. H. Spencer Lewis.

seventeen of the highest officers of the Order in Canada, United States, Mexico, and the Latin-American jurisdictions, as well as a number of officers representing many of the secret and allied activities of the organization.

The pilgrimage started from Supreme Headquarters in San Jose, California, on the evening of January 4th, and proceeded in special railway cars across the United States in a unique route touching Southern and Mexican cities and north into Canada to pick up members from various cities and take them to New York. The large party proceeded by boat to the Mediterranean and, after visiting many of the ancient cities, spent considerable time in Palestine, visiting the holy shrines of the Essenes and the Great White Brotherhood, and finally reached Egypt, where the Rosicrucian Order there prepared a number of interesting features for entertainment and instruction, including a series of initiations conducted in the ancient Rosicrucian manner, beginning at the Sphinx and the great Pyramids, with ceremonials at Lake Moeris, and culminating in a special initiation ceremony arranged by the oldest Rosicrucian lodges in Egypt in the Temple of Luxor on the Nile. From this place, the tour continued through Europe, giving the members and officers an opportunity to visit the Rosicrucian landmarks in Switzerland, France, Germany, and England. The officers of the North American jurisdiction had the pleasure of visiting, secretly and privately, the oldest of the Rosicrucian temples in Europe and meeting with many of the high officers. This unusual pilgrimage not only afforded the Imperator an opportunity to attend the official sessions, but the officers also an opportunity to make contacts seldom made by American mystics; and the initiation ceremony in Egypt whereby a Rosicrucian Egyptian lodge was instituted, composed solely of American members, was the first of its kind ever held in Egypt and will not be held again for one hundred and eight years.

The results of this pilgrimage will become highly significant as the years pass; but the one outstanding fact is that the AMORC is today the only Rosicrucian movement anywhere in the world whose principal officers and active representatives in so many jurisdictions *actually journeyed to Egypt* as in the pre-Christian Era, receiving in the ancient temple of Amenhotep IV at Luxor Rosicrucian *initiation* and Rosicrucian *acknowledgment* at the hands of officials of the oldest Rosicrucian lodges in existence anywhere in the world.* This gives the

---

*Subsequent Rosicrucian tours to Europe and Egypt were conducted by Rosicrucian officers in 1937, 1960, 1962.

AMORC a special power and an international standing which no other metaphysical organization in North America has ever had or probably ever will have.

, In 1936, the Rosicrucian Order, A.M.O.R.C., sent a motion-picture camera expedition throughout Asia Minor, Palestine, Egypt, and the countries of the Levant, to film professionally the sites of the mystery schools, the great temples, and the remains of ancient civilizations as a matter of record for the Order. A few of the places filmed included the Great Pyramids, Karnak and Luxor Temples, the Valley of the Kings and Queens, the tombs of the nobles, the great palaces of the Rameses, antiquities of ancient Thebes; the ruins of Babylon, Baalbeck, Biblos, Ctesiphon, and the Island of Lesbos in the Aegean Sea; splendid mosques of Istanbul and Pera, and centers of early culture in Italy. This was the first time that any school or society of mysticism had ever made an effort to introduce its students and members to the magnificence of the great work of these early peoples, from whom we derive so much benefit in useful and inspiring knowledge.

In 1948-49, the Supreme Council of AMORC sent three officers of the Order on a film expedition on behalf of the cultural activities of its extensive

Egyptian and Babylonian Museum. This journey took the members of the expedition to China, Thailand, India, Egypt, and Europe. By means of the Rosicrucian affiliation, temples and monasteries in India and inside Tibet were filmed. These color and sound films, as a public relations activity, have been shown to thousands of members and the public throughout the world. The Imperator wrote articles on his unique experiences in connection with the journey, not only for Rosicrucian publications but also for outside periodicals of wide public circulation.

In 1953, 1957, and 1962, further camera expeditions to the philosophical and archeological shrines of Greece, the Aegean region, the Holy Land, and the area of the Dead Sea Scrolls were conducted by the AMORC Technical Staff.

CHAPTER IX

THE INTERNATIONAL JURISDICTION
OF THE ORDER

HE original jurisdiction re-established in the United States, in 1915, has grown to become a world-wide organization. In 1934, after a meeting in Europe composed of representatives of the Order throughout the world, the jurisdiction in the Western world was extended to include North, Central, and South America. The following year, complying with the new responsibilities of the jurisdiction, the Latin-American Division of the Order was transferred to San Jose.

During the second World War, many Rosicrucian groups in Europe became inactive. In many countries, rituals and teachings had been destroyed, and these groups became dependent upon the North and South American jurisdiction. In 1946, the British jurisdiction consolidated with it* and gradually others followed, until today the international jurisdiction of the Order centers in Rosicrucian Park, San

*See following chapters for details.

Jose, California. This international jurisdiction now includes The Americas, British Commonwealth, France, Germany, Holland, Italy, Switzerland, Sweden, and Africa.

The Supreme Grand Lodge of AMORC is therefore the supreme body of the Order for this international jurisdiction, and various Grand Lodges in many parts of the world are subordinate to it. The Supreme Grand Lodge of AMORC in the United States is incorporated as a nonprofit, educational organization, and is so registered in many other countries throughout the jurisdiction. Separate jurisdictions affiliated with the international jurisdiction still function in the Scandinavian countries, Holland, and a few other parts of the world.

The Order throughout the world is known by the initials of the full name of the Order, A.M.O.R.C., which are the first letters of the words composing the full name, Ancient Mystical Order Rosae Crucis. The universal symbol of the Order is a gold cross with a *single red rose* in its center. Another symbol frequently used is an equilateral triangle with one point downward, enclosing a cross with a red rose in its center. These symbols are registered in the patent office of the United States by the Supreme Grand Lodge of AMORC, and only official Rosicrucian movements approved by the Supreme

Grand Lodge may use these symbols. These symbols and the word *AMORC* are also registered in many countries throughout the free world.

After Dr. H. Spencer Lewis had been authorized to re-establish the Rosicrucian Order in the Western world, and his powers had later been confirmed by the European jurisdiction, the responsibility for the growth of the new jurisdiction rested entirely with itself. Intercourse was continued with the International Supreme Council of the Rosae Crucis throughout the world. Teachings were transmitted in document form and by other means, from the European Order, to the A. M. O. R. C. of America, but the labors of development and expansion were confined strictly to the American administration. New policies had to be adopted to conform with conditions in the Western world, which were entirely extraneous to Europe. America knew a freedom which Europe in its most liberal period and countries never enjoyed. The secrecy, such as the European jurisdiction of the Order employed to veil its activities against abasement of its principles, was not necessary in America, and, if attempted, would arouse suspicion as to the motives of the Organization.

There existed in America, therefore, an opportunity for the advancement of the Rosicrucian teachings, with their consequent benefit to humanity, which the Rosicrucian movement had never experienced since its inception during the time of the early mystery schools. To establish and maintain lodges in just the larger cities or centers of population, as had been the custom of the Order in Europe since the time that Grand Master Frees reigned in 883-899 A. D., would be to deprive thousands of sincere American seekers of the knowledge and *light* which they sought. In every little hamlet or village, there were some who were duly prepared *inwardly* for initiation and for the Rosicrucian mystical philosophy. It would have been impossible to establish a lodge or temple in every little community, and completely furnish and equip it with the necessary ritualistic appurtenances.

At the first Convention of the A. M. O. R. C. in America, held the week of August 2, 1917, at Pittsburgh, Pennsylvania, after due deliberation by officers of the various lodges, and official delegates, a resolution was passed, establishing the *National Rosicrucian Lodge.* This Lodge was intended as a solution to the problem of expansion. It provided certain requirements, whereby a probationary, or introductory phase of the Rosicrucian teachings might be sent by correspondence to the inquirer who had met definite qualifications of membership. During the next few years considerable work was done in determining the best manner of presenting these time-honored teachings, even the elementary aspects, in a dignified and an appropriate way. From this research, there developed a system of instructions that became highly successful and won the approval of educators for its perspicuity in introducing profound subjects. The new method was accepted by the seekers for mystical truth and knowledge, in a manner far beyond the expectations of the Imperator and the Supreme Grand Master of the A. M. O. R. C. of America.

The rise and spread of Rosicrucian teachings in America became positive and rapid. Eventually, the completion of the elementary studies by the isolated Neophyte, and his desire to advance further and participate in the teachings of the Temple Degrees, as given in established Rosicrucian Lodges, renewed the old problem. A Lodge could not be established in each community where there were a few who had successfully qualified for the Postulant Degrees of the Order. Neither could these Neophytes journey with regularity to distant lodges. In 1926, Dr. H. Spencer Lewis, illustrious Imperator of A. M. O. R. C. at the time, presented the matter to a Congress of Rosicrucian dignitaries in Switzerland.*

The result was that the teachings and doctrines of the higher degrees of the Rosicrucian Order could be extended in like manner, if each Neophyte assumed certain obligations and complied with traditional ritualistic rites. After this further decision and approval, the expansion of the Rosicrucian Order of North America was still more rapid. Individuals in foreign lands, which as yet were not part of an established or recognized jurisdiction of the Rosicrucian Order, sought admission in the A. M. O. R. C. of America by this unique means. The method of maintaining a Sanctum, or "a lodge at home" was appealing. The infant American jurisdiction of the Rosicrucian Order was now able to express itself in a manner that amazed, and yet caused the Masters and Hierophants of the other jurisdictions to rejoice.

Extensive yet dignified campaigns of a public nature were conducted to draw seekers to the portals of the Temple; in other words, to shorten their time of search. In 1927, in Tampa, Florida, which was then the See of the Supreme Grand Lodge of the A. M. O. R. C. for North America, a large radio broadcasting station was erected by the Order. It

*See page 178.

was assigned the call letters of WJBB by the Federal Bureau of Communications of the United States Government. Cultural programs were extensively broadcast. Though the station was the largest in the state of Florida, no commercial activity or sale of time was conducted by it. Lectures on scientific and philosophical subjects, classical and popular music, drama, public service, addresses by prominent Government officials and educators, and a form of social service constituted its daily programs. The transmission range of the station was several thousand miles, making the name *Rosicrucian* further known, and identifying it with enlightenment and civic progress.

In 1934, the first great International conclave of the Rosicrucian Order in modern times was held in Europe. The following are excerpts from the *Rosicrucian Digest,* of November, 1934, the official publication of the A.M.O.R.C. of North America, reporting the event:

"This was not to be merely a huge assembly of initiated members of the world's oldest mystical groups. On this special occasion, only the highest officers—Imperators, Hierophants, Grand Masters, or members of Supreme Councils were to come together to meet with the representatives of the Great White Brotherhood."

"Such a great convention or congress had been anticipated for many years. It was decreed for this cycle of world activities many years ago. The first attempt in 1914 was purely of a preliminary nature, merely continuing the preliminary efforts of 1908 and earlier. In 1921 and 1927 larger preliminary sessions were held, in which our Imperator participated. In 1931 various national conventions in Europe crystallized the plans for the 1934 Congress, and again our Imperator was an important delegate."

"The opening address, made by the Venerable Imperator (of Europe) was translated into English, and it contained many and elaborate compliments to our Imperator and the work he has accomplished in North America."

"The high objects of the Convention were stressed and urged by each speaker. Among these was Fra. Wittemans, a member of the Belgian Senate, an eminent law authority, and a well-known author of a very complete history of the Rosicrucian Order, published in several languages."

"Of the many direct results, the following are the outstanding ones, of special interest to our members:" (here followed eight points, but for brevity we quote but one)

"That the Supreme Council of AMORC at San Jose, California, shall continue to be the exclusive repository for North and South America of the genuine and authorized rituals, rites, teachings, and findings of the Rosicrucian Order or Fraternity, and its allied organizations."

This, then, was another ratification of the work which the A. M. O. R. C. was accomplishing in the jurisdiction of North America, to perpetuate the ancient Rosicrucian teachings. It was further substantiation of A. M. O. R. C.'s claims to its authority, and its right to represent itself to be the perpetuator of the authentic Rosicrucian teachings in the Americas.

Of momentous importance was the Manifesto issued in 1934, which reads in part:

"Be it known that at a Convention of the Supreme Officers of the various ancient Rosicrucian Orders and affiliated bodies of the world, composing the F. U. D. O. S. I., held in Brussels, Belgium, August 13 to 18, 1934, it was unanimously decreed the S . . . . S . . . . of the A.. M.. O.. R.. C.. of North America is hereby empowered and authorized to extend its jurisdiction and exclusive authority to South America as well as to the territories and dependencies of the United States, Canada, and other possessions of North and South American countries; and that the said S. . . . S. . . . of A.. M.. O.. R.. C.. for North and South America shall have the right and authority to act as a sponsor for the establishment of Rosicrucian Lodges and Chapters, in such countries of the world not governed by any recognized Grand or Supreme Lodge or S. . . . S. . . . ,——"

This document was attested to by the signatures and seals of each of the Masters and Hierophants and dignitaries and official delegates of the august societies convening.

La Rose+Croix magazine, published for forty years, and being the official "Organe de la Société Alchimique de France et de l'Ordre Antique et Mystique de la Rose-Croix," directed by the renowned Rosicrucian alchemist, F. Jollivet Castelot, announced in its issue of January, 1935, this successful convention and the formation of the F..U..D..O..S..I.., as a victory for the mystical and hermetic orders.

In July of 1934, at an annual convention of the A. M. O. R. C. of North and South America, the Imperator, Dr. H. Spencer Lewis, dedicated the first unit of what became known as the Rose-Croix University of America.* The large, handsome, colonnaded building, of Egyptian design, housed chemistry, physics, and light and photography laboratories, classrooms, and study hall. In June of 1935 the first term of the Rose-Croix University of the American Jurisdiction began, with students enrolling in its "College of Humanities," "Fine and Mystic Arts," and "Arcane and Mundane Sciences."

---

* This and subsequent chapters of this book, excepting the Question and Answer section, were written after the transition of Dr. H. Spencer Lewis, the original author.

Rosicrucians who wished to specialize in material sciences or certain aspects of Rosicrucian arcana were given the opportunity under duly qualified instructors. Since the above date, the original building has had several annexes, which include added classrooms, a cinema studio, and a biology laboratory.

After several years of experimentation and a visit to the leading planetariums in Europe, Dr. H. Spencer Lewis had built in the year 1936 the first Planetarium containing an apparatus which he himself had designed. The magnificent domed building, with its many ingenious mechanical devices, made possible a realistic reproduction of the movement of the stars and the planets for the study of astronomy. He named it the *Theater of the Sky,* and it is indeed an appropriate title, for it portrays the cosmic roles of the cosmic bodies.

In August, 1936, the Supreme Secretary of A. M. O. R. C., Ralph M. Lewis, while on a cinema and still-camera expedition through Asia Minor, Egypt, and North Africa, attended a conference of the officers of the F. U. D. O. S. I., in Brussels, Belgium, in behalf of the Rosicrucian Order of America. He had conferred upon him an esoteric degree of the Rose Croix of Europe. The venerable Imperator of the Rose Croix Order of Europe presided at the

Initiation. He was likewise inducted into the rites of the Traditional Martinist Order of France, receiving initiation both in Brussels, Belgium, and in Paris, France. Certain Martinist documents were entrusted to him to transmit personally to the Imperator of A. M. O. R. C. of America upon his return.

Again, in August of 1937, another International Convention of the Rose Croix was called for Brussels, Belgium, and the F.U.D.O.S.I., with its allied bodies, convened at the same time. The sessions were presided over by *three Imperators*. Signal honors were conferred upon many of the various dignitaries. Dr. H. Spencer Lewis, having had conferred upon him the various degrees of the Traditional Martinist Order years previously, was now appointed Regional Sovereign Legate for the Martinist Order in the United States and its territories and dependencies. He was given charters empowering him to re-establish the rites of Martinism in the United States, as they had descended from its Illustrious Venerable Grand Master, Louis Claude de Saint-Martin. The charters and decrees were signed by the rightful successor to *Papus,* first president of the Supreme Council of the Traditional Martinist Order, with Sanctuary in France.

The versatility and organizing genius of Dr. H. Spencer Lewis is also seen in the fact that he organized and directed the establishment of the Rose-Croix Research Institute and Sanitarium, which first accepted patients in the Spring of 1939. For years, he relates in Rosicrucian literature, he had dreamed of having a center for healing, where the various established systems of treatment could be used in conjunction with the Rosicrucian methods of healing for the alleviation of suffering and, by study and research, to advance the therapeutic arts. Through the financial assistance of Rosicrucian members throughout the world, the Institute was equipped with the latest instruments and apparatuses for the treatment and study of disease. Many Rosicrucian principles were employed in the design and lighting of patients' and treatment rooms and in the development of unique facilities.*

In June of 1939, the Supreme Secretary, Ralph M. Lewis, on behalf of the Imperator, dedicated the Rosicrucian Research Library. Of Egyptian design and modern in every respect, the library employs the latest systems of filing and contains several thousand volumes on such subjects as occultism, mysticism, Rosicrucian philosophy, the arts, history, and the

---

*This activity was suspended a few years after the transition of Dr. H. Spencer Lewis.

sciences. It is for the exclusive use of Rosicrucian members, who, even though they cannot attend, can avail themselves of its research facilities by correspondence.

In August of 1939, the Scandinavian Lodges of the Rosicrucian Order held an International Convention in Malmo, Sweden, under the jurisdiction of the A. M. O. R. C. Grand Lodge of Sweden. A National Convention of the Danish Grand Lodge preceded this in Copenhagen by a few days.

In the same month, officers of the F.U.D.O.S.I. convened for the consideration of important pending matters, one of which was Dr. R. Swinburne Clymer's false claims to Rosicrucian authority and a renewal of his scurrilous attack on the Imperator and the organization of A.M.O.R.C. of North and South America.

The delegates to these two respective conclaves representing the A. M. O. R. C. of North and South America were the Imperator's personal representative, James R. Whitcomb, who had on previous occasions met with officers of the F.U.D.O.S.I. in their Congresses, and the Sovereign Grand Master of A. M. O. R. C. of America.

On August 13, 1939, in Brussels, Belgium, a Decree, written in the French language, was signed and sealed with the esoteric emblems and insignia of office of the Imperator of the Rose Croix of Europe and given to James R. Whitcomb to transmit to the Imperator of A. M. O. R. C. of America. It is now in the repository of the Order in San Jose, California. The document reads in part:

"It is inevitable that the AMORC, the only Organization in the Western world perpetuating the teachings of the R+C that have been transmitted by written or spoken word by the R+C instructors, become the target of evil forces working through isolated individuals or organizations, who would attempt to put obstacles in its way and to curtail its progress.

"Therefore, in due Assembly in Brussels, Belgium, on this 13th day of the month of August, in the year 1939, we, members regularly elected of the Supreme Council of the F.U.D.O.S.I., after due examination of the elements of appreciation in the case that has been submitted to us, do proclaim that Reuben Swinburne Clymer, who does profess to perpetuate the true and ancient Rosicrucian teachings in America and who assails the character of the Hierarchy of AMORC, and who seeks to stalemate its progress, is in no wise recognized by us as having any Rosicrucian authority.

"We do also proclaim that the so-called International Confederation of Rosicrucians which R. Swinburne Clymer purports to exist in Europe, and with which he claims to be associated and deriving certain articles of authority, is in no wise recognized by the R+C Orders and Fraternities of Europe that are affiliated to the F.U.D.O.S.I. In our opinion, the above-mentioned Confederation, is a clandestine organization that is illegitimate in its function, and does not give any initiatique guaranty."

The Convention of the Rosicrucians in Sweden concluded about one month prior to the beginning of the second World War. It made possible the putting into order of their affairs, before the anticipated calamity which befell them. They presented several documents, or Manifestoes, to James R. Whitcomb, delegate of the Imperator of America, attesting to their unity with the Rosicrucian Order, A.M.O.R.C., of North and South America, and deploring the clandestine movements which sought to interfere with the work of the authentic Order. A manifesto signed by the Grand Master and Grand Secretary of the Rosicrucian Grand Lodge of Denmark, in Copenhagen, on the 14th of August, 1939, on the occasion of their National Convention, and referring to the above-mentioned delegates of A.M.O.R.C. from America, states:

"Their stay, even though brief, has done much to cement the two jurisdictions—theirs of North and South America and ours of Denmark—into closer understanding and mutual support, for the spread of the ancient Rosicrucian teachings, which we perpetuate as a Sacred Heritage."

The Supreme Council of the Martinist Order and Synarchy of the United States was legally incorporated on the 3rd day of August, 1938, in the State of California. Having been fraternally affiliated with the Rosicrucian Order in Europe for nearly two centuries, it was proper that it should also be closely aligned with the Rosicrucian Order's activities in America. The transition of the Illustrious Imperator of America, Dr. H. Spencer Lewis, occurred on Wednesday, August 2, 1939, at 3:15 P.M., Pacific Standard Time, in San Jose, California, the Sovereign Sanctuary of the A.M.O.R.C. for North and South America. It therefore became necessary that his authority as Sovereign Legate and Supreme Grand Master of the Traditional Martinist Order be transferred to another. By order of the Supreme Council of the Traditional Martinist Order of France, which was the sponsor of the American jurisdiction, the charters and manifestoes of authority granted to Dr. H. Spencer Lewis were then transferred to his son, Ralph M. Lewis. Ralph M. Lewis was his traditional and *elected* successor as Imperator for the Rosicrucian Order, A.M.O.R.C., for North and South America. He was duly elected and proclaimed Imperator by the Board of Directors of the Supreme Grand Lodge of A∴ M∴ O∴ R∴ C∴, on Saturday, August 12, 1939. He had served as Supreme Secretary of the Order for fifteen years. On this same occasion, Cecil A. Poole, who had been the former Director of the Latin-American division of AMORC, was elected the Supreme Secretary and Treasurer of the Rosicrucian Order, AMORC, for North and South America. A proclamation to the entire membership of the Grand Lodge of the Order, announcing these changes, was made in the October, 1939, issue of the *Rosicrucian Digest,* the official periodical of the A.M.O.R.C.

On March 7, 1940, in an official communication to the Imperator, Ralph M. Lewis, the Acting Secretary of *The International Supreme Council of the Order Rosae Crucis,* Mademoiselle Jeanne Guesdon, notified him as to the results of an election held by that body, as follows: "I must say that they are all unanimous in their wish to have you, Ralph M. Lewis, as President of the International Supreme Council."

CHAPTER X

DEVELOPMENT AND EXPANSION
IN FRANCE

HE traditional Rose-Croix of France, following its custom of small secret bodies
meeting as Rosicrucian lodges scattered
throughout the nation, was rapidly dimin-
ishing by its own admission. The two great
World Wars had taken their toll of the members.
The economic plight in which France found herself
following these catastrophes had made it impossible
for the Order of the Rose-Croix to conduct even the
most conservative program for rehabilitation and
expansion. Furthermore, at the International Conventions held in France and Belgium, which are
referred to in the previous chapters, it was expressed
by the Venerables of the Rose-Croix that the more
liberal times, the growth of population, and the increasing opposition to the enlightened tenets of the
Order by materialistic movements necessitated
changes in its policies.

The seclusion in France of the Rose-Croix was
denying many persons worthy of the teachings
knowledge of where it existed and how to contact

it. The Venerables, therefore, realized the need for a revitalization of the Rosicrucian Order in France. They had previously given the AMORC of the International Jurisdiction, with its See in America, their approval to extend the teachings privately to qualified initiated members for study in their home sanctums (p. 196). They desired that the same modern methods used by AMORC in America be adapted to France. However, they believed themselves not prepared to accomplish this purpose. Consequently, it was decided that the AMORC of America should establish a Grand Lodge of its own in France and extend the Order's activities in like manner in that nation. This modern activity would be concomitant with the remnants of the old Rose-Croix.

For some years, Mlle. Jeanne Guesdon, a native of France, residing in Villeneuve-Saint-Georges, a suburb of Paris, had been a member of the Rose-Croix, France, and a scholar of the traditional esoteric orders. She was recognized as a brilliant student of mysticism and metaphysics and had functioned for several years as liasion officer between Dr. H. Spencer Lewis and certain of the mystical bodies of Europe. In addition to these activities, she was also a member of the AMORC of America and was highly enthusiastic about its expansion program and its preparation and manner of presenting the Rosicrucian teachings.

Dr. H. Spencer Lewis, the incumbent Imperator of AMORC, conferred with Mlle. Guesdon with regard to her assisting in the voluminous and tedious work of translating the modern form of the teachings and rituals into the French language. She agreed to undertake this task and immediately began her voluntary labor of love. The Imperator's transition occurred before much of this work could be accomplished. Following this, World War II and the Nazi occupation of France further inhibited Mlle. Guesdon's efforts. After World War II, the newly presiding Imperator, Ralph M. Lewis, journeyed to France to confer with Mlle. Guesdon, and preparation for the AMORC in France was renewed with vigor.

In July, 1954, Mlle. Guesdon attended the International Rosicrucian Convention in San Jose and conferred with the Supreme Council there. She passed through transition suddenly in March, 1955, after a short illness. The work of AMORC in France had, nevertheless, been established by her sacrifice, with the full cooperation and further direction of the Imperator, Ralph M. Lewis.

Although a tremendous amount of effort had been expended, the organization of AMORC in

France was still in a rudimentary stage. The transition of Mlle. Guesdon produced a temporary state of confusion. She had clerical assistance but no one as yet qualified to succeed her as Grand Secretary of AMORC, France. The Imperator was obliged to fly to France from America to try to surmount the difficulties. He was able to engage the voluntary services of the illustrious Grand Master of Sweden, Albin Roimer, who generously divided his time between his own jurisdiction and that of France in order to administer the latter's affairs temporarily. This he did with true Rosicrucian fraternal spirit. It became obvious, however, that this arrangement was not expedient and would actually interfere with the functioning of both the French and Swedish jurisdictions.

For some time, Mlle. Guesdon had been impressed with the sincerity, intelligence, and dynamic personality of a young frater of the Order, Raymond Bernard, who lived in southern France. She had corresponded with the Imperator of AMORC with regard to him, expressing the hope that sometime she might prevail upon Frater Bernard to assist her with the burdens of the growing Order in France. She passed through transition before realizing this hope. The Imperator, conscious of the necessity of a permanent direction for AMORC France and a need to release the Grand Master of Sweden from his burden, approached Frater Bernard. In 1955, they met in conference with Grand Master Roimer in France. Not long after this conference, Frater Raymond Bernard assumed the office of Administrator of AMORC France. But with the transition of Mlle. Guesdon, there was now actually no official officer of AMORC in France.

The confidence in Raymond Bernard which Mlle. Guesdon had expressed, as well as the favorable impression he had created upon the Imperator, were substantiated by his efforts. He not only had a highly evolved mystical consciousness and mentality, but an excellent academic education and administrative ability. He followed the instructions of the Imperator of AMORC explicitly, adopting the modern methods proposed to him. As a result, the AMORC France membership grew rapidly. AMORC France now has a Grand Lodge and includes in, its jurisdiction Switzerland, Belgium, and the French-speaking countries of North and West Africa and elsewhere throughout the world. Pronaoi and chapters of enthusiastic members soon grew into lodges.

Mlle. Guesdon began the work of AMORC in France in her own home and even constructed a small administration office on her property. She bequeathed this property to AMORC France, in trust for the Supreme Grand Lodge of the Order. The AMORC in France, however, soon outgrew the original facilities and has since acquired much adjoining property at Villeneuve-Saint-Georges. It has beautifully landscaped these properties and built modern administration buildings, as well as an attractive temple for ritualistic and ceremonial work.

In July, 1959, Frater Bernard, with his wife Yvonne, who has ably assisted him, attended the International Rosicrucian Convention in San Jose. While there, he was duly vested with the honorable title and authority of Grand Master of AMORC France. The ritualistic stole and emblems of office were conferred upon him in the Supreme Temple in Rosicrucian Park. Subsequently, in 1962, in company with other officers of the Order, he again journeyed to the International Convention in San Jose. Also, he has traveled extensively throughout Europe and Africa, speaking to subordinate bodies of AMORC France.

With the growth of AMORC membership in Europe and with the realization that comparatively few of the many members could journey to America for an International Convention, a similar convention was decided upon for Europe. The first of these modern conclaves was held in Geneva, Switzerland, in October, 1960. The second of these biennial conventions was held in Paris (1962), with hundreds of Rosicrucians from throughout Europe in attendance. Grand Lodge officers of Sweden, Denmark, Holland, England, and Italy were present. The Imperator presided at the memorable event. A similar function of magnitude was held in Paris in September, 1964.

CHAPTER XI

OTHER WORLD-WIDE ROSICRUCIAN
ACTIVITIES

NDER direction of Frater Albin Roimer, who succeeded the noble efforts of his predecessor, Frater Anton Svanlund, as Grand Master of Sweden, the Order is flourishing in that country of relatively small population. The Grand Master, Albin Roimer, has also patterned his activities in Sweden after the structure of the AMORC International Jurisdiction. The Grand Lodge of AMORC Sweden, being subordinate to the Supreme Grand Lodge, which has its See in the United States, has acquired an extensive property and building in Skelderviken. Its administrative offices and temple are located there.

In recent years, several of the books of the Rosicrucian Library have been translated into the Swedish language and are beautifully printed and publicly circulated. In 1960, Grand Master Roimer attended the International Rosicrucian Convention in Paris and, subsequently, conferred with the Imperator and other Grand Lodge officers of Europe and elsewhere. Under Frater Roimer's direction, lodges and chapters have been established throughout Sweden.

Following World War II, an effort was made by the Imperator of AMORC to reactivate the defunct Rosicrucian Order in Italy. The former illustrious Grand Master, Dunstano Cancellieri, a true venerable, resided in Tunisia during World War II. While there, he translated many of the English monographs into Italian. It was also his intention to rehabilitate the Order in Italy along the lines of AMORC elsewhere. He passed through transition before accomplishing his splendid purpose.

In more recent times the work of Italy has been reactivated under the guidance of Grand Master Raymond Bernard of France. With the decline of religious opposition in Italy the work is again progressing well.

The Italian Grand Lodge has published Rosicrucian books in the Italian language and periodically issues an official journal, *Il Rosacroce*, which is similar in design to Rosicrucian periodicals published by other jurisdictions of the Order.

During World War II, the eminent Grand Master of AMORC in Great Britain, Raymund Andrea, found it impossible to continue the activities of the Order in that jurisdiction. It was not possible to prepare and disseminate the teachings. The Imperator then decreed that the Grand Lodge in the United States should assume the responsibility of forwarding all Rosicrucian instructions to the members throughout the British Isles. At that time, British members could not remit dues to the United States because of government restrictions on exporting funds from their country. Upon an appeal from the Imperator, American members rallied to the cause and personally donated an amount sufficient for defraying the expense of carrying the memberships of the British fratres and sorores for several years.

At the conclusion of the war, correspondence between the Imperator and Grand Master Raymund Andrea revealed the fact that the British jurisdiction was not able to continue its prewar activities. Consequently, in the fall of 1945, the Imperator journeyed to Bristol to confer with Frater Andrea on this momentous matter. After a thorough analysis of the situation, a manifesto was signed on October 25, 1945, which stated in part: "The jurisdiction of the Rosicrucian Order (AMORC) of Great Britain and the Ancient, Mystical Order Rosae Crucis (A.M.O.R.C.) of North and South America, shall, after the date finally appearing below, coordinate, for the joint dissemination of the Rosicrucian teachings and the rehabilitation of the

Rosicrucian Order in England, Ireland, Scotland, and Wales."

Subsequently, administrative problems made it necessary that an administration office be established in London by the Supreme Grand Lodge for the better servicing of members' needs. By 1965, the work had grown to such proportions that the office in London was moved to Bognor Regis in Sussex, where the Order now enjoys a greater expanded area for work in a modern office building. There it is known as the Commonwealth Office, serving the British Commonwealth of nations.

Although there were many subordinate bodies of AMORC in Great Britain, none were ritualistically qualified to confer all of the traditional full degree initiations. Therefore, this essential phase of the Rosicrucian work in modern times was being neglected, a condition which the Imperator greatly deplored. A ritualistic initiatory team for Great Britain was finally established in London by the Imperator. This team has conferred the beautiful initiations upon several hundred members in recent years. The meticulous manner and observance of details in the performance of these initiations have been most creditable to the team.

Since the beginning of the middle of the twentieth century, conclaves of the Order, as conventions, have been held annually in London. Because of excellent organization and programming, these conventions have become exceptionally successful. They attract Rosicrucians not only from throughout the British Isles, but also from elsewhere in Europe and from America and Africa.

In Denmark, Holland, and Germany, the activities of the Order had been seriously disrupted by World War II.*

---

*In Denmark, recovery was slow, but steady under the guiding hand of Grand Master Arthur Sundstrup and his co-worker, Grand Secretary Kaj Falk-Rasmussen who at this writing are still discharging their duties from the Grand Temple in Copenhagen.

The recovery in Holland accompanied the more rapid economic and cultural revival there. Under the leadership of Grand Master Jan Coops and his able Secretary, Harm Jongman, the Order grew in size and stature. Today, the Grand Lodge of Holland is ably directed by Edward van Drenthem Soesman who serves as its Secretary-General in The Hague.

In Germany, the traditions and historical aspects of the Order gave impetus to its regeneration there after World War II. Now one of the strongest Rosicrucian bodies in Europe, it has its Grand Lodge in Baden-Baden, directed by its Secretary-General Wilhelm Raab.

Chapter XII

PROGRAM OF DECENTRALIZATION

ROSICRUCIAN activity in Latin America had increased considerably. The Latin-American peoples were generally psychologically more disposed to the study of mysticism and the philosophical teachings of the Order than most other nationalities. Pronaoi, chapters, and lodges sprang up throughout Central and South America in the decades following World War II. Extensive promotional campaigns of a dignified and educational nature further stimulated interest in the Rosicrucian Order on the part of the general public. The entire Rosicrucian library of books was eventually translated into Spanish and disseminated throughout the Latin world. All the teachings, rituals, and instructions of the Order were made available in the Spanish language.

The Imperator and Frater Cecil A. Poole, then the Supreme Secretary, made numerous journeys to Rosicrucian subordinate bodies in the Latin countries. They took part in their conclaves (conventions) and conferred with their officers. Qualified members were selected as Grand Councilors voluntarily to assist officers and members in the respective countries of Latin America.

With the increased political turbulence throughout the world in the middle years of this century, the Supreme and Grand Lodges of AMORC were faced with many administrative problems. It became more and more difficult to serve the members in some of the distant countries. A serious inconvenience to student Rosicrucians was the delay of surface mail for many weeks. The difficulty of exporting monies from some countries imposed an additional economic problem upon the member and the Grand Lodge which served him from the United States. The high cost of labor for administration in the United States, plus the need to maintain dues at a much lower rate for members in countries elsewhere, made a program of decentralization advisable.

Membership in Brazil had grown rapidly. However, its distance from the Grand Lodge and its dependence upon the facilities of that body increased administrative problems. The Imperator, accompanied by the Grand Regional Administrator, Arthur C. Piepenbrink, made a journey to Brazil to confer with officers of the lodges in Rio de Janeiro and São Paulo. As a result of these conferences, two Brazilian members, Maria Moura and

Jose de Oliveira Paulo, were delegated to translate the monographs and all doctrinal and ritualistic materials into the Portuguese language, a truly stupendous undertaking.

Finally, in 1956, the Grand Lodge of Brazil was regularly organized and established. It became subordinate to the Imperator and the Supreme Grand Lodge. Notwithstanding a number of serious economic cycles within Brazil, AMORC flourished. Maria Moura was duly appointed Grand Secretary of AMORC Brazil and Jose de Oliveira Paulo, Grand Treasurer. Under their capable direction and organization, with the full cooperation of the Supreme Grand Lodge, a magnificent administration building was erected to house the growing staff in Curitiba, in the State of Paraná.

In September, 1964, adjoining the Brazilian administration building of like size and design, a splendid Grand Lodge temple of Egyptian-style architecture was completed. Officers of the Supreme Grand Lodge in San Jose personally participated in the formal and inspiring dedication ceremony of the temple upon the occasion of the Brazilian National Rosicrucian Convention, held for the first time in that same year. Grand Secretary Maria Moura had journeyed to San Jose in 1963 to attend the International Convention of the Order. While there, she conferred with other Grand Lodge officers from throughout the world and made arrangements for the temple dedication. In October, 1970, the Imperator again visited Brazil, this time to dedicate another addition to the growing building complex in Curitiba, a large and beautiful auditorium, named for Dr. H. Spencer Lewis.

Similar circumstances which had necessitated the establishment of the London Administrative Office and the Grand Lodge Administrative Office in Brazil now existed in other parts of the world. Members in Australasia, that is, Australia and New Zealand, were likewise plagued with long mail delays because of distance and complicated international regulations. It became apparent that some immediate relief must be provided them if the Order is to grow in those countries. The Imperator and other officers had on several occasions visited Australia and New Zealand officially. Their conferences with officers of the Order in those lands emphasized the urgency of the need for remedial measures.

In November, 1963, the Imperator, went to Auckland, New Zealand, to establish an administrative office to serve Australasia. This meant the dissemination from there of all of the doctrinal and other literature issued by the Order to the nations of that area. In 1969, the Australasian office was moved to Melbourne, Australia. Previous weeks of delay in receiving the study material they needed was thus eliminated for members.

Further conferences of the Supreme Council of AMORC during 1964 resulted in resolutions passed by that body that other administrative offices should be established in such areas of the world as circumstances required. Thus the international aspect of the Order was intensified, its single legal jurisdiction being retained even though a decentralization of its activities was necessary. But no longer could one central headquarters provide all of the facilities for world-wide membership. However, the See of the Order in San Jose for many reasons would need to conduct exclusively certain activities which could not be duplicated elsewhere.

On May 4, 1966, the Order suffered the loss of Mrs. H. Spencer Lewis who passed through transition on that date. She had carried on a great number of labors begun by her husband, Dr. H. Spencer Lewis, and served to complement his mission in giving impetus to the Order's growth in the twentieth century.

Her absence left a vacancy on the Board of Directors which was subsequently filled by Raymond Bernard. Upon his election, he was assigned the coordination of Rosicrucian activities in Europe, assuming the role of Supreme Legate for Europe.

Other changes in the roster of officers were necessitated by the retirement of Grand Master Rodman R. Clayson and Grand Secretary Harvey Miles, and by March, 1971, the full complement of officers at the See in San Jose read as follows:

SUPREME GRAND LODGE

Ralph M. Lewis	Imperator
Cecil A. Poole	Treasurer
Arthur C. Piepenbrink	Secretary
Raymond Bernard	Legate for Europe

GRAND LODGE

Chris. R. Warnken	Grand Master
James R. Whitcomb	Grand Secretary
Robert E. Daniels	Grand Treasurer

A Few Words To Those Who Are Strangers

If you, Reader, are not a member of the Rosicrucian Order, we wish to take this opportunity to greet you, and to thank you for the opportunity of placing in your hands this history of the organization with the questions and answers which further explain the ideals and purposes of the Rosicrucians.

There are two ways by which this book may have come into your hands: first, through the courtesy of some member or interested person who has believed that you would be interested in its contents; second, through your own acts whereby you have either purchased this book or borrowed it from the shelves of some public library. If the book is in your hands through your own act, it is an indication of your curiosity or your interest.

We hope, therefore, that you have found in the history of the organization such information as satisfies your desire for facts, and that we have introduced ourselves to you sufficiently well to have you know us better and appreciate the real traditions of the Order as compared with the false beliefs and misunderstandings which have been so prevalent in the past centuries. There is, perhaps, no other organization in the world that has been so greatly misunderstood as the Rosicrucians.

We cannot say that all of this is due to a brief or mysterious presentation of the history, for much is also due to the writings of many novelists, who have found in the history and traditions of the Order the basis for many weird, fantastic, and romantic plots. As stated in the Introduction to this history, there was a time when such stories as *Zanoni,* by Bulwer-Lytton, served their purpose in revealing the existence of the organization, but surrounded it with a cloak of mystery and fantasy, which left the seeker for its portals doubtful of any success in his search. For almost a century, the fictitious mystery which enveloped the Rosicrucian Order has been dispelled by the illumination of research and publicity.

Today, nearly all modern and comprehensive encyclopedias give an accurate account of the purposes and history of the A.M.O.R.C. Even abridged dictionaries refer to it, and the veil of mystery as to its existence and activities has fortunately been lifted. Excellent accounts, brief but authoritative references to the Rosicrucian Order of the past and present, may be found in the 14th Revised Edition of the *Encyclopaedia Britannica, New Standard Encyclopedia, Winston's Cumulative Loose-Leaf Encyclopedia and Dictionary, Modern Encyclopedia, Webster's Unabridged Dictionary, Funk & Wagnalls' Unabridged Dictionary,* and many others.

The Rosicrucian Order today throughout the world represents a movement of high idealism and high purpose. It has become a public movement among men and women of repute and wide affairs and is no longer the closed council for restricted membership. Its work has broadened into many channels and its place in the evolution of modern civilization has become fixed and well recognized.

If you are interested in knowing more about the

organization or desire to share its teachings and practices, you are cordially invited to make further inquiry; and if your expressions are sincere and it is apparent that more than curiosity prompts your inquiry, you will receive that encouragement which will enable you to have your desires fulfilled.

In order that the Secretary may competently take care of your inquiry and know that you have already read this book and are familiar with the facts contained therein, he would thank you to address your letter to the department name given below.

Scribe L. L. C.

Rosicrucian Order, AMORC
Inquiry Department
Rosicrucian Park, San Jose, Calif. 95114, U.S.A.

INDEX

A

Abydos, 15
Adfar Alexandrinus, 87
Administration building, 186
Africa, 184, 192, 213
Against Apion, 79
Agrarian rites, 35
Agrippa, Cornelius Heinrich, 90
Ahmose I, 43
Akhnaton, 57. See: Amenhotep
   IV
Albertus Magnus, 89
Alchemy, 172
Alcuin, 94
Alexandria, 75, 76
Al-Farabi, 89
Amasis, 87
Amenhotep I, 43
Amenhotep II, 52
Amenhotep III, 52
Amenhotep IV, 46-47, 52-60, 61,
   63-64, 77, 79, 188
America, First cycle of Order in,
   92, 138, 155, 163-168
America, Second cycle of Order
   in, 169-190
American Rosae Crucis, 19
American Rosicrucian seal, 51
Ammon, 56, 57, 63, 69
Ammonius Saccas, 80
AMRA, 67, 95
Anaximander, 72, 88
Anaximenes, 88
Ancient Mystical Order Rosae
   Crucis, 178. See: Rosicrucian
   Order, AMORC
Andrea, Johann Valentin, 91,
   115-116, 124-125
Andrea, Raymund, 217-218
Anima artis transmutationis, 89
Antiochus, 88

A

Apostles, 84
Aquinas, Thomas, 89
Aristotle, 88
Arnaud, 95-97
Arndt, Johann, 90
Arnold of Villanova, 89
Ashmole, Elias, 91
Athens Lodge, 88
Aton, 55, 57
Atonamen, 64
Australia, 224-225
Avicenna, 89
Aye, 69

B

Bacon, Sir Francis, 90, 125, 163
Bacon, Roger, 89
Balzac, Honoré de, 93
Barrett, Francis, 93
Beissel, Conrad, 14, 92
Belgium, 213
Bellcastle-Ligne, Count, 176
Bernard, Raymond, 212-214, 217,
   225-226
Blake, William, 93
Boehme, Jacob, 90
Book of the Dead, 42
Books, AMORC, 180, 184, 216,
   217, 221
Books claiming to be Rosicrucian,
   149-151, 152
Books: S.R.I.A. and Fellowship,
   179
Boyle, Robert, 91
Brazil, 222-223
Breasted, James Henry, 66. See:
   History of Egypt
British Commonwealth, 184, 191-
   192
Brown, Edward H., 149
Bruno, Giordano, 90
Bubastis, 68-69

INDEX

Budge, E. A. Wallis, 40, 42
Busiris, 87

C

Cagliostro, Count Alessandro, 92, 173
Calid, King, 87
Camera expeditions, 189-190, 201
Campanella, Tommaso, 90
Canada, 181, 184, 187
Cancellieri, Dunstano, 217
Carmel, Mount, 82, 84
Cassel, Germany, 108, 113, 125
Castelot, François Jollivet, 93, 172, 200
Central and South America, 184
Charlemagne, 89, 94-96, 100
Christians, 121-122
Christine Church, 83-85
Christus of the Rosy Cross, 108
Cicero, 88
Clavicula, 89
Clayson, Rodman R., 226
Cloud on the Sanctuary, 93
Clymer, R. Swinburne, 151-159, 204-206
College of Rites, Lyons, 173
Colotes, 88
Commonwealth Administrative Office, 219
Concerning the Cause, Principle, and One, 90
Confessio Fraternitatis, 115
Constant, Alphonse Louis, 135, 146
Constitution of AMORC, 180-181
Convention:
    AMORC (1917), 180-181, 194
    AMORC (1934), 200
    International, Brussels, 202, 209
    International, Europe, 1934, 181-182, 197-200
    International, France, 209
    International, Geneva, 214-215
    International, Malmo, 204-206

Convention *(Continued)*
    International, Paris, 215
    International, San Jose, 214
    International, Switzerland, 182, 196
    International, Toulouse, 182
    National, Brazil, 223
    National, Denmark, 204, 206-207
    National, London, 219-220
Coops, Jan, 220
Corelli, Marie, 93
Council at El Amarna, 66-67
"Council of Seven," 146
Council of Thutmose III, 47-48, 50
Council, Supreme, 61, 97, 99, 177, 198, 208
Cross, 85-86, 118-122
Cross and rose, 58, 122, 178
Crotona, 72
Cruce Signatorum Conventus, 120
Crux ansata, 58
Cycle, 108-year, 103-106, 109, 116-117, 166-167, 188

D

Dalton, Dr. John, 93
Daniels, Robert E., 226
Dante Alighieri, 89
De Alchimia, 89
De Anima, 88
De occulta philosophia, 90
De vita aeterna, 91
Debussy, Claude, 93
Decree of 1939, 204-206
Dee, Dr. John, 90
Degrees, Neophyte and Temple, 195-196
    Twelfth, 49
Demetrius, 76
Democritus, 88
Dendera, 37
Denmark, King of, 120
Descartes, Rene, 91, 171
Deutsche Gottesfreunde, 160
Diogenes Laërtius, 71-72

INDEX

Discours de la Méthode, 91
Divine Comedy, 89
Documents and manifestoes, 48-51, 106, 167, 177, 199-200, 204-207, 218-219
Dowd, Freeman B., 148-149
Dramas, Mystical, 37

E

Eckartshausen, Karl von, 93
Egypt, 99
  Origin of Order in, 20, 33-60
  Pilgrimage to, 186-189
Egyptian: Lodge, 188
  Prince with apron, 15
  Science, 38-39
El Amarna, 57-58, 61, 64, 66, 68, 70, 75, 78
Elijah, 82
Elizabeth I, 120
Empedocles, 88
Encausse, Dr. Gerard. See: *Papus*
Encyclopedia of Rosicrucian science and arts, 89
Encyclopedias and dictionaries, 228
England, 99, 106, 129-136, 167-168, 171, 217-220
English Physitians Guide, 91
Ephrata Cloister, 14
Epicurus, 88
Equinox, Spring, 44
Esoteric knowledge, 40-42
Essenes, 79-84, 122, 187
Euclides, 88
Euphrates: or the Waters of the East, 91
Europe, 184
Evelyn, John, 91

F

Fama Fraternitatis, 91, 113-116
Faraday, Michael, 93
Feast of spring equinox, 44
Fees, 184
Fidelis, Fra, 19-20

Figulus, Benedictus, 62, 91
Flamel, Nicholas, 89
Flanders, 171
Fludd, Dr. Robert, 90
France, 94-100, 106, 167-168, 169-178, 182-183, 192, 209-215
Franklin, Benjamin, 92, 165
Frederick, Duke of Württemberg, 121
Freemasons, 25-26, 71, 98, 128-144, 168, 180, 183
Frees, 97-98, 194
F.U.D.O.S.I., 10-12, 154-158, 199-202, 204-206
Funk, I. K., 174

G

Gabalis, Comte de, 171
Galilee, 82, 84
Garasse, 171
Gaultius, 171
Geber, 89
Geheimnisse, 92
Gentiles, 82-84
German Pietists of Pennsylvania, 164-166
Germany, 99, 100-101, 105-106, 108, 110, 111-125, 160-161, 167-168, 171, 192
God, 55, 69
Goethe, Johann Wolfgang von, 92
Golden Calf, 91
Gould, Sylvester Clark, 141-143, 173-174
Grand Councilors in Latin America, 221-222
Great Britain, 171, 217-220
Great White Brotherhood, 17, 20, 23, 26, 43, 75, 77, 79-86, 155, 187, 197
Great White Lodge, 33, 173
Greeks in Egypt, 61-62, 71
Guesdon, Jeanne, 208, 210-214
Guillem, St., 95

INDEX

H

Hanover Lodge, 120
Hartmann, Dr. Franz, 93
Harvey, Dr. William, 91
Hatshepsut, 44, 52
Heidelberg Grand Lodge, 164
Heindel, Max, 156, 159-162, 173, 179
Heliopolis, 75, 77, 79, 82
Helmont, Jean Baptiste van, 91
Helvetius, Dr. John Frederick, 91
Henry IV, 120
Heraclitus, 88
Hermarchus, 88
Hermes Trismegistus, 63-65, 78, 87
Hermetic Order of the Golden Dawn, 171
Herodotus, 37-38
Heydon, John, 91
Hieroglyphic Monad, 90
Hieroglyphics, 77
Hieronymus, Sar, 11, 157
Hiram Abif, 70
His Exposition of the Hieroglyphical Figures, 89
Histories of the Order, 24-25
Historisch Verhael, 170
History of Egypt, Breasted, 46, 54, 60
History of Egypt, Manetho, 77-79
History of the Order, Toulouse, 99
Holland, 106, 182, 192
Holy League, 118
Hubbard, Elbert, 93, 174-175
Hu-ram-abi of Tyre, 70

I

Illuminati, 49, 66, 72, 182
Imperator of Europe, 198, 201, 205. See: Hieronymus, Sar
Imperators, Three, 202
India, Legates from, 175-177
Initiations in Egypt, 187-188

Initiatory team in Great Britain, 219
International Confederation of Rosicrucians, 157-158, 205-206
Irenaeus Agnostus, 91
Italy, 171, 192, 217-218

J

Jacob Boehme Lodge, 164
Jean de Meung, 89
Jefferson, Thomas, 92, 165
Jennings, Hargrave, 146
Jesus, 83
Jewels, 51, 106
Josephus, Flavius, 79
Journal of the American Medical Association, 156
Julius Africanus, 79
Jursidiction of AMORC, 181-182, 191-192, 198-199, 218-219

K

Karnak, 44, 50, 53, 56
Kelpius Cave, 13
Kelpius, Johannes, 92, 164
Kheri Hebs, 40, 45, 75
Khufu, 37
Khunrath, Heinrich, 90
Komensky, Jan Amos, 91

L

Lasalle, 177
Latin-America, 187, 221-224
Latin-American Division, 191
Le Brun, Dr. Clement, 9
Leade, Jane, 91
Leibnitz, Gottfried Wilhelm von, 92
Leipzig Grand Lodge, 101
Leonteus, 88
Leontium, 88
Levi, Eliphas. See: Constant, Alphonse Louis
Lewis, Dr. H. Spencer, 9, 11, 27-31, 153, 157, 158, 174-177, 182-183, 186-189, 193, 195, 198, 200-203, 207, 210-211, 225

INDEX

Lewis, Mrs. H. Spencer, 225
Lewis, Ralph M., 31, 201-203, 207-208, 211-212, 224, 226
Library, German Rosicrucian, 90
Little, Robert Wentworth, 131-132
Lodges, Rosicrucian, 66-67, 194, 195
London Administrative Office, 219
Louis Lambert, 93
Louis XIII, 171
Lully, Raymond, 89
Lumen de Lumine, 91
Luxatone, 28
Luxor, 53, 54, 56, 187, 188
Lyons, 98, 173
Lytton, Edward George, Lord Bulwer-, 93

M

Ma, 41-42
Maat, 66
Magus, 93
Maier, Dr. Michael, 90
Mallinger, Jean, 157
Manetho, 77-80
Manifestoes. See: Documents
Maria Hebraeae, 87
Martinists, 92. See: Traditional Martinist Order
Mause, 100
Mazzini, Giuseppe, 93
McKenzie, Kenneth R. H., 132-135
Meditationes de Prima Philosophia, 91
Members of the Order, 87-93
Membership qualifications, 184, 194-196
Mena, 87
Mene, 48
Metaphysica, 88
Metrodorus, 88
Metropolitan College, S.R.I.A., 134
Mexico, 181, 184, 187

Miles, Harvey A., 226
Militia Crucifera Evangelica, 85-86, 117-125
Miller, Peter, 92
Miris, 87
Moeris, Lake, 187
Monastery, Rosicrucian, 98-99
Monastic orders, 57-58
Monotheism, 55, 77-80
Montpellier, 99
Moray, Sir Robert, 91
Moses, 79-80
Moura, Maria, 222-223
Mysterium Magnum, 90
Mystery schools, 15, 34-41, 50, 76, 77, 79, 80, 86, 164, 189, 194
Mystical Life of Jesus, 83
Mysticism, 80

N

Name of the Order, 48-50, 133, 145, 170, 178, 183, 192
Naometria, 90, 121-123
National Rosicrucian Lodge, 194
Naude, 171
Nazi occupied countries, 183
New Atlantis, 90, 125, 163
New Thought, 151
New York Institute for Psychical Research, 175
New Zealand Administrative Office, 224-225
Newton, Sir Isaac, 92
Ney, Marshal Michel, 93
Nigidius Figulus, 88
Nimes, Rosicrucian monastery, 98-99
North America, 169-186
Norton, Thomas, 90

O

Obelisk of Thutmose III, 50, 51-52
Occult Review, 144
O'Donnell, John, 93

INDEX

On the True Theologia Mystica, 92

Opus Majus, 89

Oration on the Dignity of Man, 90

Ordinall of Alchemy, 90

Ordre Antique et Mystique de la Rose-Croix, 200

Ordre Cabbalistique de la Rose-Croix, 171

Ordre de la Rose Croix, 170

Organizations, Modern esoteric, 173

Orient, 167

Osirian mysteries, 35-38, 41

P

Palgrave, W. G., 146

Papus, 202

Paracelsus, 90

Parmenides, 88

Pasquales, Martinez de, 92, 171

Paulo, Jose de Oliveira, 223

Persecution, 167-168

Philadelphia Lodge, London, 164

Philadelphia, Pennsylvania, 13, 155, 164-166, 174

Philalethes, Eugenius, 91

Philo, 88

Phonaire, 99

Pico della Mirandola, 90

Piepenbrink, Arthur C., 222, 226

Pietists, 164

Pike, Albert, 137

Planetarium, 29, 185, 201

Plato, 77, 80, 88

Plotinus, 80-81, 88

Plutarch, 36, 38

Poemander, 64-65

Poole, Cecil A., 208, 221, 226

Portus Tranquillitatis, 91

Principia, 92

Printing, 107, 111-112

Profundis, 49

Ptolemy Philadelphus, 76-78

Publicity, 186, 196-197

Puppets, 37

Pyramids, 187

Pythagoras, 71-73, 87

R

Ra, 42, 77

Raab, Wilhelm, 220

Radio station, AMORC, 196-197

Rameses II, 63

Randolph, Paschal Beverley, 145-152, 156

Raymond VI, 89

Red Cross of Rome and Constantine, 133

Reincarnation, 104, 108

Richelieu, 171

Ripley, Sir George, 90

Rituel de la Maçonnerie Egyptienne, 92

Roerich, Nicholas, 93

Roimer, Albin, 212, 216-217

Roman Catholics, 172

Roman de la Rose, 89

Rosacroce, Il, 217

Rosarium Philosophorum, 89

Rose and cross, 58, 122, 178

Rose-Croix, 200

Rose-Croix Catholique, 172

Rose-Croix Research Institute and Sanitarium, 203

Rose-Croix University, 185-186, 200-201

Rose, Jacques, 171

Rosenkreuz, Christian, 21, 106-110, 114, 116

Rosicrucian:

    Books claiming to be, 149-152

    College, Nimes, 99

    Digest, 172, 184, 197-198, 208

    Doctrines, 80

    Egyptian Museum, 15, 185

    Fellowship, 156, 159-162, 179

    Literature, 107, 111-116

    Name. See: Name of the Order

    Order, AMORC, 153-155, 157-158, 178, 226-229

INDEX

Rosicrucian (*Continued*)
   Order, AMORC, Authority of,
      181-182, 198-199, 204-206
   Order, Origin of, 18, 20-21,
      24, 25, 33-60
   Park, 185-186
   Research Library, 186, 203
   Research Society, 174
   Teachings, 150, 184, 193-196,
      198-199, 210-211, 217-218,
      221, 223
*Rosicrucians and Their Teach-
   ings*, 151
Rosicrucians, List of, 87-93
Rosicrucians, Suppression of, 183
Roycrofters, 174-175
Rubinstein, Anton, 93
Russia, 167

S

Sachse, Julius Friedrich, 93, 163-
   167
Saint-Martin, Louis Claude de,
   92, 171, 202
Sais, Priests of, 77
Salomon, 67-71
Sanctum, 196
Scandinavia, 192, 204
School, Charlemagne's, 94-96
Science Building, 9, 185, 200-201
Science Museum, 185
Seal of the Order, 50-52
Secrecy, 23-24, 42, 48-50, 183,
   193
Sedir, 149, 151
Seneca, 88
Sesostris, 87
Sethon, 87
Seti I, 63
Sex regeneration, 152
Shishak I, 68, 69
Simandius, 87
Sinai, Mount, 79
Sirius, 41
Sistrum, 39
Societas Rosicruciana in America,
   143-145

Societas Rosicruciana in Anglia,
   130-146, 171, 179
Societas Rosicruciana in Cana-
   diensis, 136-137, 139
Societas Rosicruciana in United
   States of America, 136-143,
   174
Societe Alchemique de France,
   200
Socrates, 88
Soesman, Drenthem, 220
Solomon's Temple, 25. See:
   Salomon
Solon, 71, 77, 88
Sothis, 78
Spain, 167, 171
Spinoza, Baruch, 91
Steiner, Rudolph, 159-160, 173
Studion, Simon, 90, 119-123
Sue, Eugene, 93, 170
Sum of Perfection, 89
Sun worship, 55, 69, 77
Sundstrup, Arthur, 220
Supreme Grand Lodge, 192
Svanlund, Anton, 216
Sweden, 192, 216-217
Switzerland, 167, 171, 176, 192,
   213
Symbols: Akhnaton's, 58
   AMORC, 133, 178, 192-193
   S.R.I.A. and Fellowship, 179

T

Temples: Brazil, 223
   Carmel, Mount, 84
   Egypt, 36-37, 41-42
   El Amarna, 57-58, 61, 70
   European, 188
   Helios, 82
   Lodge rooms and, 184
   Neith, 77
   Rosicrucian, 28
   Solomon, 69-70
   Supreme, The, 185
Thales, 77

INDEX

Theano, 72
Thebes, 57, 68-73, 75, 95
Thehopset, 53
Themis Aurea, 90
Themista, 88
Therapeuti, 80, 81
Three Principles, 90
Thutmose I, 43-44
Thutmose II, 44
Thutmose III, 44-48, 50-52
Thutmose IV, 52
Tia, 53
Tibet, 84
Tomb of C. R-C., 106-108
Toulouse, 96-98, 173, 176
Tours to Egypt, 188
Tractatus Apologeticus, 90
Traditional Martinist Order, 202, 207
Trithemius, Johannes, 90
Truth, 66
Twelve Gates, 90

U
United States, 187

V
Vaughan, Thomas, 91
Verdier, 182

W
Waite, Arthur Edward, 131-132, 134, 146-148, 155-156, 163, 165
Wandering Jew, 93
Warnken, Chris. R., 226
Weigall, Arthur E. P., 55
Westcott, W. Wynn, 130, 132, 133, 140
Whitcomb, James R., 204-206, 226
White, William Henry, 132
Wilcox, Ella Wheeler, 93, 175
Wirtembergis Repertorum der Litterator, 121-122
Witt, Dr. Christopher, 92
Wittemans, Frans, 153, 171, 198
World Wars I and II, 183, 191, 211, 217, 218, 220
Worms Lodge, 100
Wren, Sir Christopher, 92

Y
York College, 139

Z
Zanoni, 93, 227
Zola, Emile, 170
Zoroaster, 83
Zweytes Silentium Dei, 90

ORDER FROM YOUR FAVORITE BOOKSELLER OR CALL FOR OUR FREE CATALOG